THE CUSTER COUNTY SHERIFF'S LOG

Life, Death, Shenanigans and Tomfoolery in the Black Hills of South Dakota, 2005-2014

Seth Thompson

SST Solutions Group, LLC

Copyright © 2024 Seth Thompson

All rights reserved.

No part of this book may be reproduced, or stored in a retrieval system, or transmitted in any form or by any means, electronic, mechanical, photocopying, recording, or otherwise, without express written permission of the publisher.

Cover Design by Cody Karas

ISBN 9798340963802

Published by SST Solutions Group, LLC
Box 209
Hot Springs, SD 57747
United States of America
Terra

CONTENTS

Title Page	
Copyright	
Dedication	1
Well...How Did I Get Here?	2
1: Only In The Black Hills	5
2: Bison Are Dangerous	11
3: Tourons	13
4: Flashlights Are Funny	18
5: Hold My Beer	20
6: The Pringle Cows and Other Crazy Critters	40
7: Awesome Alliteration	54
8: Is The Truth Out There?	57
9: All Over The Road	66
10: It's Four-Twenty Somewhere	78
11: Y'all Ain't Gonna Believe This	84
12: The Moral Of This Story Should Be Obvious	110
13: Name That Tune	118
The Night Shift	120
One: Welcome To the Night Shift	121
Two: Dealing With a Flashlight Problem	124

Three: Warning- Reading This Column May Cause Drowsiness	127
Four: The Street Cop's Superstition Sweepstakes	130
Officer Lumpy Joins the Night Shift	133
One: A Preemptive Apology For 2010	134
Two: You Say You Want a Revolution?	137
Three: Lumpy Says Goodbye to the Crown Vic	140
Four: One Out of Five	143
Five: Lumpy Gives Fire Directions	146
Rally Of The Damned	149
1. Friday	150
2. Saturday	152
3. Sunday	154
4. Monday	156
5. Tuesday	158
6. Wednesday	160
7. Thursday	164
8. Friday	166
9. Saturday	168
Street Life	173
Death In a Cow Pasture	174
Two Worlds	177
Free Advice	180
About The Author	183

DEDICATION

To my long-suffering wife Kim, for going it alone on a lot of late nights, weekends and holidays while I was pushing a patrol car around the county...and for being my first reader and best critic...and for putting up with all my shit.

WELL...HOW DID I GET HERE?

The author circa 2003, in his Chevy Impala, a.k.a. the "police-package clown-car".

I've always been a writer. I wasn't always a cop.

Writing for the high-school magazine, a couple of small indie papers, and churning out a lot of mostly unpublished short fiction and some unfinished novels was the sorry sum total of my writing career through high school and college. I had started college as a journalism major, but graduated with a criminal justice degree and (mostly) never looked back.

In 2005, I was a fairly-new, but fairly-salty (or so I thought) sheriff's deputy in Custer County, South Dakota. I was one of eight cops who were the primary (and often only) first responders in a county that was bigger than some east-coast states. I was working the overnight shift and three of my five work nights were pretty lonely, as I was the only cop awake and in a patrol car from eleven at night until seven in the morning. I wasn't complaining very much- I was still a bright-eyed youngster who craved the usual police action.

One day, our lieutenant called me into his office and said he had decided to turn over the weekly newspaper log to me. His reasoning was that I had studied journalism in college and my case reports seemed to have the least number of typos and misspellings in them. Later, I realized that reading all the calls and case reports and typing a summary for the local paper, the *Custer County Chronicle*, was also a lot of work. This may have been a big factor in his decision to lay it off on an unsuspecting rookie.

As I eased into my new assignment, I figured out some ways to streamline the process. I also began to get bored with it. Anyone who knows me well can tell you that boredom causes my sense of the absurd to swell and my inner smart-aleck to surface. So, I began to add my own spin to what I was writing. A simple weekly newspaper list of police activity gradually became *The Sheriff's Log*.

Much to my surprise, people liked it. While out and about, doing "regular old police work", many kind readers would let me know how much they appreciated the column. Some sent copies to relatives in other places. The column was mentioned on the *Late Show with David Letterman*, and I was interviewed by other media outlets about what the *Log* was and what made it tick. The *Chronicle* began publishing a top-twenty compilation of their favorite *Log* entries every year. The paper and I would get angry calls and emails when the column didn't appear due to over-work, vacation, or space limitations.

So, here's a heaping helping of the hilarity and insanity that I chronicled in the *Chronicle,* from the beginning in 2005, through 2014, when I left the Sheriff's Office for a few years. Also included are selected opinion page and humor columns that appeared as "The Night Shift", as well as some previously-unpublished accounts of my misadventures between the times I was employed as a "real" cop, and my musings on the nature of life, death, and justice on the street.

SETH THOMPSON

Please note that the following entries are in the order in which they first appeared in the paper. They are not chronological, which may account for strange sequences of times and dates.

-Seth Thompson

1: ONLY IN THE BLACK HILLS

Long-time residents of the Black Hills can tell you that certain things are unique to our area: the scenery, the wildlife, the characters that populate the place. We also invite a lot of folks from the rest of the world to check it all out during the summers (and hopefully leave us a lot of their money), which also makes for some stupefying situations you won't find elsewhere.

10:42 p.m.: It all started with a dispute over a late check-in at a campground on Flynn Creek Road. Soon, the situation spiraled out of control with words exchanged between two males, punches thrown and taken, threats made to push a vehicle off the property with a backhoe and a counter-threat made with a .38 revolver. Luckily, both males were apparently bluffing and no shooting or backhoe-ing occurred. You can't make this stuff up, but it's still surprising when otherwise law-abiding adults choose to "act the fool" like this.

***

A late-breaking springtime storm blanketed Custer County with lots of wet snow during an April weekend, causing numerous accidents and hazardous driving conditions. Anyone who doesn't consider the Black Hills to be real mountains is in for a shock, as they definitely have mountain weather. The results are as follows:

11:10 a.m.: A deputy assisted two motorists after their vehicle slid off Highway 87, in Custer State Park.

12:15 p.m.: Reports were received of a jack-knifed truck and trailer on Highway 40, west of Hermosa. A deputy checked the area, but found no vehicles in peril.

1:41 p.m.: A two-car accident was reported on Montgomery Street, in Custer. No injuries were reported.

5:21 p.m.: Deputies responded to an accident with injuries near the junction of Highway 16 and North Pole Road. A vehicle apparently struck a state snowplow, and then collided with another car. Four people were transported to the hospital by ambulance. One person's injuries were reportedly serious. Highway 16 was closed to traffic for several hours while the mess was cleaned up. The accident is under investigation by the Sheriff's Office and the Highway Patrol.

6:53 p.m.: A passer-by was cited for careless driving at the scene of the accident on Highway 16, after he passed a stopped patrol car at a high rate of speed, without stopping.

8:46 p.m.: A vehicle collided with a road sign on South Eighth Street, in Custer. No injuries were reported.

Whew.

***

10:21 a.m.: It's a sure sign summer is around the corner when the lost hiker calls start coming in from the Harney Peak area. Search and Rescue units spent several hours locating a lost Minnesota man, then bringing him back to civilization. He was cold and dehydrated, but survived his night in the woods.

12:57 p.m.: A person was reportedly very upset that the Custer County Courthouse was closed, due to the "No Travel Advisory" in the area. The person apparently went home after registering their complaint.

7:17 p.m.: Possibly lost hikers were reported in the Bear Mountain area. Although the reporting person said the two hikers had a map and told her they knew where they were, she still believed they were lost. A deputy checked the area, but did not find them. Either they are still up there, or they really knew where they were.

3:42 a.m.: A confused semi-truck driver drove down Sylvan Lake Road and realized his mistake when he confronted the low-ceilinged Hood Tunnel. A deputy and a Highway Patrol trooper assisted him with backing his rig up the hill to the nearest turnaround. This happens more often than you might think.

10:38 a.m.: Deputies gave friendly advice to a member of an outlaw motorcycle club at a semi-popular Custer convenience store. The motorcyclist was apparently smoking while putting gas in his bike. This may have been the least risky activity he engaged in all day.

8:07 a.m.: A hot air balloon landed on Highway 385, blocking part of the highway. The support crew soon deflated the big gas bag and got it out of the way. No injuries were reported.

7:56 p.m.: The first serious snow storm of the season brought the usual motorized mayhem to Custer County. The centerpiece of the chaos was the traditionally trapped trucks weighted with wood chips in Hell Canyon, on Highway 16. Deputies, snow plows, wreckers, and a Highway Patrol trooper all cooperated to rescue the hapless behemoths and their bewildered drivers. Again. Elsewhere, with a few exceptions, most drivers proved their prudence by staying home in the rotten conditions. Scattered power outages were reported, but most were quickly taken care of.

3:26 p.m.: A man called to report he had been hiking overnight on Iron Mountain Road, and was now trapped behind the closed snow gates there. The State Department of Transportation was contacted to free the hapless hiker.

6:28 p.m.: Rare petrified wood and other rocks were reportedly stolen from behind a downtown Custer business. The incident is under investigation, concentrating on anyone sneaky and strong enough to make off with a ton or so of rocks without being seen.

11:58 a.m.: A local car reportedly backed into a Canadian military vehicle, in downtown Custer. The only injuries were apparently to Canada's national pride.

1:01 p.m.: Trespassers were reported at a mining operation just north of Pringle. A deputy warned the out-of-state scofflaws to stay off the claim.

4:09 a.m.: A semi-truck was reportedly stuck on Highway 87, north of Sylvan Lake. A deputy checked with the driver and found the truck was not stuck, but the driver was waiting for daylight to back out of the area and turn around. Since the truck would not fit through the Hood Tunnel, a few hundred feet in front of it, backing out was the only option. The driver was not able to explain how he had missed the numerous signs warning of the tunnel ahead.

10:18 p.m.: Someone called 911 on their cell phone to report some kind of fires going "somewhere between Custer and Crazy Horse". The person was unable to give a better location because they were "driving too fast to see" and apparently unwilling to stop. The fires turned out to be controlled burn piles set by foresters. Signs had been posted on the highway advising motorists of this fact, but apparently the reporting person was going too fast to see those, too.

8:22 p.m.: Deputies assisted two members of a quaint little motorcycle club with broken-down bikes, on Mount Rushmore Road, in Custer. Replace the word "club" with "gang affiliated with the Banditos", and you'll get the idea.

1:49 p.m.: "A very dangerous biker" was reportedly riding recklessly on Highway 36, near Hermosa. He was described as wearing a shirt with "STURGIS" on it, and a black bandanna on his head...like all the others. The boorish biker wasn't found.

10:54 a.m.: A lost pager was reported somewhere in Custer State Park. If you hear a mysterious beeping noise while hiking in Bear Gulch, you may have found it.

10:25 a.m.: Two out-of-staters were reportedly beating on each other at a tourist campground just west of Custer, on Big Pine Road. Once deputies arrived and sorted out the story, no one wanted to press any charges. The two combatants were apparently disagreeing over whether a bathroom was closed for cleaning or not.

6:06 p.m.: Someone called in to report a member of an outlaw motorcycle club, wearing their club jacket and "driving not so good", in the Hill City area. The person was not able to further explain how the greasy gear jammer was not "driving so good", or why they were reporting their concerns to the wrong county.

12:49 p.m.: Another pair of out-of-town tourists were reportedly beating on each other, at the gas pumps of a semi-popular Custer convenience store. After deputies arrived, the two fighters decided not to press charges against each other. The fisticuffs were apparently sparked when one person told the other to turn his vehicle off while he was fueling it, and the other told him to mind his own business. Sounds like the "vacation spirit" to me.

11:17 a.m.: Deputies, search-and-rescue personnel, park rangers, state troopers, ambulances and a helicopter all converged on the Custer State Park workers dorms, lights flashing, sirens wailing, and tires screeching, after a report of a person falling from high rocks in the area...only to find that someone's dog had fallen from the rocks, instead. The dog was treated for its injuries and was expected to recover.

7:59 a.m.: Reckless drivers were reported in the Wolf Lane area; possibly chasing after a hot-air balloon. Neither vans nor balloons were found in the area.

4:18 p.m.: Marauding Mongolians were reportedly pillaging... er, selling things in downtown Custer without a tax license. A deputy sent them packing.

6:58 p.m.: A person called from a porta-potty near the Custer sign to report they were trapped by a hailstorm. It was not clear what the person expected deputies to do for them. The person was advised to stay put until the hail stopped.

10:26 a.m.: Two naked people were reportedly sitting on a rock, near North Pole Road. The disrobed duo apparently left the area or put their clothes on before anyone got there.

8:14 a.m.: Vandalism was done to the "CUSTER" sign above the town of Custer. Some alterations had been done to make it read "LUST", instead. Some information was received about the lusty hooligans, and the investigation continues.

6:43 p.m.: Lost jewelry was reported on the roadside of Highway 16, near Crazy Horse. The owner apparently lost the items while trying to wave at passing motorists to slow down, because of a deer grazing in the ditch.

4:34 p.m.: More transient cleaning product salesmen were reported, on Sidney Park Road. A deputy checked on them and eventually arrested one, a 45-year-old Ontario, California male, for an active warrant. The summer season has been rough on traveling salesmen in the Custer area.

2: BISON ARE DANGEROUS

While the Internet apparently discovered the Custer State Park bison herd just a few years back, after the notorious "de-pantsing" of a female tourist, locals have been rolling their eyes and chortling about various bison/tourist antics for years.

9:40 p.m.: As the old saying goes: "Mess with the bull, and you get the horns". A car messed with a large bull buffalo near Legion Lake, suffering horn-inflicted damage. Both the buffalo and driver were apparently unhurt.

10:32 p.m.: A man was reportedly "surrounded by buffalo" in the Wind Cave area. He was found some time later, safe and sound. The hooligan herd hoofed it out of the area before deputies and park rangers arrived.

2:56 a.m.: More buffalo bullying was reported by an out-of-state tourist, on Highway 87, near Blue Bell Lodge. Apparently, the hoofed hooligans were blocking the road and would not let her pass. A deputy went there and cleared the way with his siren.

6:54 p.m.: Reports were received of a buffalo "treeing" someone near the Game Lodge, in Custer State Park. No unruly bison, nor any treed tourists were found in the area.

6:09 p.m.: Deputies assisted with a fire call, near Blue Bell Gate, in Custer State Park. The small blaze was apparently caused by a vehicle detouring off-road to avoid a tourist/buffalo jam. The fire was quickly put out, but charges are pending on the driver.

7:32 p.m.: A tourist was savaged by a buffalo, near Legion Lake Lodge. The tourist suffered serious injuries to their leg, after coming too close to take pictures.

4:45 p.m.: Buffalo were reportedly menacing motorists on Highway 79, near Lame Johnny Road. Their owner was called to stop the madness.

3: TOURONS

Most visitors to the Black Hills show up for all the right reasons and use their vacation to decompress and relax, while keeping their wits about them and treating the locals (and each other) nicely. However, some visitors make the mistake of expecting things to be just like "back home", or resort to turning their brains completely off, with predictable results. Those folks are often referred to with a contraction of the words "tourist" and "moron".

1:32 p.m.: Tourists from New Jersey called to report their car was stuck in the mud at the Fairburn Cemetery. A tow truck was dispatched to free them. They were unable to explain just what they were doing there.

8:41 p.m.: An out-of-town tourist flagged deputies down to insist that downtown Custer restaurant owner be arrested for "child abuse". The tourist said that his child had fallen out of a possibly defective seat at the restaurant and this constituted child abuse. The short answer to this is: no, it actually doesn't. The man refused any medical treatment for his child. However, the man later called 911 to tell his sorry story...and got the same answer, once again.

4:33 p.m.: Deputies and park units helped a wayward tourist back their motor home down from the Hood Tunnel, on Highway 89. Apparently, it was too large to fit.

10:38 p.m.: Deputies checked on some suspicious tourists at a Custer golf course. They were apparently just doing some night putting.

5:03 p.m.: It Must Be Summer, Part I: A truck was reportedly stuck in the Hood Tunnel, on Highway 87. However, a deputy checked the area and found nothing crammed in the crevice in question.

2:28 p.m.: It Must Be Summer, Part II: A large motor home grounded its frame on a Highway 87 switchback curve, just north of the Hood Tunnel and jammed up traffic on the whole road. Various agencies worked together to free the hapless behemoth. It is not clear how the occupants of the RV planned to squeeze it through the tunnel, had they cleared the curves.

10:53 p.m.: A tourist called in to report someone was banging on the windows and doors of her cabin, just east of Custer, on Highway 16A. The mysterious "burglar" turned out to be her brother, who had apparently locked himself out.

10:25 a.m.: Two vehicles collided at low speeds on Badger Clark Road. Apparently, an out-of-state visitor was backing up to look at an animal by the roadside, without using his mirrors. No injuries were reported.

12:01 p.m.: An out-of-state traveler called in to report a herd of horses she thought was about to escape their pasture just off Highway 79, near Fairburn. When questioned why she thought this, the traveler said the horses were standing near an open gate with a cattle guard, "looking like they were about to get out". A deputy checked the area, but found no wandering horses.

1:22 p.m.: Someone was reportedly dumping water from their RV into a gutter, on Sixth Street, in Custer. A deputy checked, but found no dumping going on. He did give them some pointers on using less than four parking spaces.

12:49 p.m.: Out-of-state tourists were reportedly trying to dig up a large quartz rock and cart it away, just inside Custer State Park, near the Gordon Stockade. A deputy went there, but the would-be rock hounds had already made good their escape.

12:29 p.m.: A deputy went to a campground north of Custer, to deal with a seasonal employee who was rudely trying to claim his final paycheck before he left the state. After calming the situation, the deputy took the 41-year-old Oregon man down the road and bid him a fond farewell.

6:32 p.m.: Out-of-state tourists called in to report their minivan was broken down on the Wildlife Loop Road, in Custer State Park. The tourists were apparently nervous about their surroundings, requesting law enforcement, as well as a tow truck, because "it's the Wildlife Loop". No buffalo, antelope or jackrabbits attacked them before a park ranger got there but the twitchy travelers called back at least once, wanting to know when the law would arrive to rescue them.

12:02 p.m.: Two tourists slid off the icy Wildlife Loop Road in their woefully under-equipped car. Luckily for them, they were rescued by deputies and a helpful tow truck driver.

9:13 p.m.: Deputies dealt with a suspicious vehicle at Comanche Park Campground. One of the Canadian (and still suspicious) occupants earned a ticket for an open alcoholic beverage in a motor vehicle.

1:38 p.m.: An irate tourist called to report sewage backing up into his vehicle at a campground north of Custer, and he was not given a refund when he complained. This turned out to be a civil matter.

6:15 a.m.: Tourist trouble was reported by cell phone, somewhere in Wind Cave National Park. The travelers from Illinois said they took a wrong turn trying to reach Custer, and then got lost. To add to their woes, a herd of buffalo "surrounded" them, and they believed they were almost out of gas. A deputy went there to help, but did not find the troubled travelers, who had apparently resolved their situation somehow.

5:39 p.m.: A "strange man" from out-of-state reportedly made a mess in the dining room of a Custer restaurant, on Fifth Street.

He then said something about having just been in a mental hospital, left the building and disappeared soon after.

8:32 p.m.: Someone called to complain about the service they received at a Custer restaurant. Though this kind of thing isn't usually a police matter, a deputy went there and smoothed the whole fracas out.

9:25 a.m.: Someone reported motel guests had smoked in a non-smoking room, in the Custer area. Not surprisingly, this is a civil matter.

3:44 p.m.: Someone called to complain about an inconsiderate bus driver who was apparently crowding a buffalo crossing the road, in the Wildlife Loop Road area. The matter was referred to the bus company.

8:56 a.m.: A deputy investigated unwanted guests at a campground on Iron Mountain Road. The crass crew craftily crept away without coughing up any cash for the campground. This incident was decided to be a civil matter.

5:03 p.m.: A woman from out-of-state called 911 to report she was being "harassed by a big black park ranger", at Game Lodge Campground, in Custer State Park. As it turned out, the park ranger in question was not involved in any harassment but was there to investigate a report of the woman allowing a small child to drive a car around the campground. Despite the pathetic 911 call, the park ranger continued his investigation and he and a deputy eventually ejected the problem people from the area.

9:35 p.m.: It must be summertime: a deputy ejected tourists from a downtown Custer grocery store parking lot, after they set up camp there in their RV.

2:48 p.m.: A tourist called in on his cell phone to breathlessly report he was following a vehicle south of Custer that resembled one involved in a missing child report in Wyoming. Contact with Wyoming authorities found that the report actually involved an overdue adult motorist, not a missing child. It didn't matter, anyway, as the reporting person didn't get the vehicle's license plate number or figure out what state it was from.

4:22 p.m.: A badly-driven car was reported on Highway 16, north of Custer. A deputy found the suspect vehicle and dealt with the foreign tourist driver, who apparently was sober but not very good at driving in America.

9:25 p.m.: Deputies, search-and-rescue team members, and an ambulance all scoured the Mount Coolidge area for a tourist who was on wandering on foot in the woods after an argument with his wife. The tourist was found, safe and sound, after a short search. If only he had learned the magic words: "You're right, honey."

2:28 a.m.: A deputy and a state trooper attempted to assist an agitated and intoxicated female whose husband had apparently run off with another woman (and their car), at a downtown Custer motor lodge. Her other half was not heard from again.

2:23 p.m.: An upset Spanish-speaker called to report... something, on the 911 line. A helpful park ranger who did "habla" checked on the person and found they were all right.

4: FLASHLIGHTS ARE FUNNY

Few things seem to arouse the suspicion of small-town residents faster than the appearance of someone using a flashlight after dark. Cops find this hilarious, as they know that actual bad guys crave the shadows and darkness to do their deeds, and rarely light their way while they're doing it.

The call that started it all, as repeated on the now-defunct Late Show With David Letterman:

10:10 p.m.: Suspicious people were reportedly doing something with flashlights, by the side of North Fifth Street, in Custer. A deputy checked and found the people were not suspicious, but merely Canadian.

***

10:06 p.m.: Suspicious people were reportedly shining flashlights around an abandoned Custer sawmill. Deputies searched the area, but found no suspicious flashlight shiners about.

7:32 p.m.: A mysterious hitchhiker was reportedly shining a blue flashlight at passing cars, on Highway 16, near Hell Canyon. His blue beacon apparently attracted a ride, as he had disappeared before a deputy arrived.

5:32 p.m.: Someone in a black pickup was reportedly "flashing red and blue lights and a flashlight" at passing cars, on Highway 16, north of Custer. Deputies responded to the area but the possible police poser had vanished.

8:45 p.m.: Suspicious people with flashlights were reported in a pasture on Silver Star Lane. The mysterious flashlight people were not found.

10:18 p.m.: A suspicious man carrying a beer and wearing a light on his hat was reportedly walking around a cartoon-themed campground, in Custer. This is not generally a crime.

5: HOLD MY BEER

Not surprisingly, cops everywhere deal with a lot of drunk people. Lots of those people probably wouldn't have gotten themselves into the pages of this column without the help of copious quantities of alcohol.

2:17 a.m.: A deputy attempted to stop a man riding a horse on the shoulder of Highway 79, near Hermosa. The man, who appeared to be intoxicated, refused to stop and would only identify himself as "Jose Cuervo". The man and horse then attempted to get away, leading to a short car/horse pursuit. The man and horse were not able to elude the deputy. Eventually, another deputy arrived to assist, and the 22-year-old Kyle man was arrested for disorderly conduct, and obstructing an officer. The horse was not charged.

3:29 a.m.: An intoxicated female called 911 from Hot Springs to request she be sent a taxi to give her a ride. The Hot Springs Police Department was called, since the female had an active warrant for her arrest. The HSPD was more than happy to give her a ride…to jail.

Thursday, October 31st

10:27 p.m.: An intoxicated male wearing a hot dog costume was reportedly found sitting in the back of the wrong parked car, behind a downtown Custer tavern. Another bar patron, dressed in a skeleton outfit, apparently attempted to apprehend the dirty dog, who escaped on foot, but was soon rounded up by a deputies and eventually taken home. No charges are likely to be filed in the incident.

***

The Happiest Night of Their Lives:

8:59 p.m.: A deputy assisted a Custer State Park ranger with a report of an intoxicated and unruly person at an outdoor wedding party near the Game Lodge. By the time the officers arrived, the person was gone.

10:39 p.m.: Deputies and park rangers were back at the wedding party to check on reports of a stolen and wrecked golf cart, and damage to parked vehicles. A park ranger attempted to quiet the gathering, as they were being very noisy after quiet hours. A group of party-goers got mouthy and threatening with the officers, which resulted in more park rangers and more deputies showing up. Eventually, the drunken crew left the area with a lot of bad noise, but none of them apparently felt up to "taking a shot at the title".

3:05 a.m.: Deputies and park rangers returned to the Game Lodge area for a report of an intoxicated person sleeping in the wrong rental cabin after kicking the door in to gain entry. By the time everyone arrived, the disoriented drunk had disappeared. Other damage was done to the cabin and surrounding picnic tables.

The final tally for this evening of drunken and debauched damage:

One mangled golf cart.
One dented pickup truck.
One twisted power pole guy wire.
One broken door.
Two burned picnic tables.
Lots of empty beer cups.
Lots of pounding hangovers.

The incident is under investigation, and charges may be pending on several suspects.

**

1:53 a.m.: Unknown suspects absconded with the popcorn machine from a Custer bar, just before closing time. The incident is under investigation.

11:59 p.m.: Deputies responded to an alarm at a Custer bar and found a broken door, but no other damage. It turned out that the broken door was caused by a bar patron who did not believe that the bar had closed early.

6:19 p.m.: Deputies responded to Highway 40, east of Hermosa, for a report of a body lying in the ditch. The "body" turned out not to be dead, but dead drunk. The extremely intoxicated man was taken to the detoxification facility in Rapid City.

5:00 p.m.: An off-duty reserve deputy called the dispatch center to report a possible drunk driver leaving a restaurant near Hermosa. The deputy also observed the two occupants switch seats in the front of the vehicle before they left the restaurant. While the deputy was still on the phone, the vehicle collided with another vehicle at the junction of Highways 79 and 36. Both vehicle occupants had to be extricated from the first vehicle, and were subsequently arrested for DUI, as both had control of the vehicle for a short period of time. The occupant of the other vehicle received minor injuries.

11:32 p.m.: A deputy responded to a report of a stranded motorist on Highway 79, south of the Fairburn turn. When he arrived, he found the vehicle had three intoxicated people in it. After an investigation, the deputy arrested the driver, a 32-year-old Rapid City woman, for driving under the influence of alcohol, no proof of insurance, and no valid driver's license. He also arrested on of the passengers, a 40-year-old Pine Ridge woman, for an active warrant. On the way to the jail, one of the suspects vomited all over the backseat of the deputy's patrol vehicle. Yuck.

***

12:33 a.m.: An intoxicated male called in from somewhere in Custer demanding his power be turned back on. When told he needed to contact the power company, the male replied that was "too much work" and insisted the dispatchers turn his lights back on, before eventually hanging up.

2:26 a.m.: A deputy assisted a Highway Patrol trooper with the arrest of a 55-year-old Custer male for DUI, at Seventh and Crook Streets, in Custer. It turned out to be the same man who made the call about his lights being turned off. He was apparently on the way downtown to pay his bill.

***

5:14 p.m.: A 26-year-old Rapid City man was arrested on Highway 79, South of Buffalo Gap, for driving under the influence of alcohol. At first, he gave deputies a false name. After he was booked into the Pennington County Jail, the man admitted his real name. He was then also charged with false impersonation, driving with a revoked license, and was served with six outstanding warrants, including three felonies.

5:31 p.m.: Custer County deputies became involved in a vehicle pursuit that started near Hill City. A Pennington County deputy attempted to stop a possible drunk driver in the Hill City area. The driver refused to stop and continued south on Highway 16. A Custer County deputy used a tire deflation device (a.k.a. Stop Sticks) on the suspect's vehicle. The suspect swerved and attempted to hit the deputy, but was unable to stop him from successfully deflating two of the suspect's tires. The suspect ran off the road about two miles later, as deputies converged on his location. The suspect refused to cooperate with deputies, and they were forced to use a TASER device to gain compliance from him. The suspect, a 61-year-old Nisland man, suffered charges in both counties, including aggravated assault, DUI second offense, eluding, reckless driving, driving with a revoked license, and a nasty hangover when he woke up in jail.

11:55 a.m.: A deputy assisted the Highway Patrol with a possible fight in a vehicle, just north of Hermosa. The vehicle in question was found abandoned, unoccupied, and reeking of alcohol. It is unknown who was fighting or why.

2:12 a.m.: Deputies went to a Custer bar, for a possible medical emergency. When they arrived, they found a drunken individual who had been asked to leave the bar, and wanted a ride home in an ambulance or police car. He was told to find his own way home.

4:53 p.m.: An intoxicated man repeatedly called, demanding a deputy come to his residence. It turned out the man lived in another county, and was calling the wrong dispatch center.

6:13 p.m.: Deputies and a highway patrolman investigated a report of an intoxicated man who was shoplifting from a Custer grocery store. When the 55-year-old Custer man was found, he was arrested for shoplifting, as well as drunk driving.

3:36 a.m.: A deputy stopped to check on three people walking by the side of Highway 385, north of Custer. The people told him that they had been given a van ride by an intoxicated man who was driving very recklessly. The man had apparently hit several road signs before his hitchhikers asked to be let out. The deputy investigated the matter further, and eventually found the alleged van driver at a residence in Custer. The 24-year-old man was arrested for DUI. Other charges may be pending on the man.

11:20 p.m.: A deputy found an intoxicated person walking by the side of Highway 16, west of Custer. The tipsy man was given a ride home. Apparently the man was having trouble staying on the sidewalk. At least he wasn't driving.

7:19 p.m.: A report was received of a man lying in the ditch next to Highway 79, near Hermosa. When a deputy arrived, the 39-year old Red Shirt man was found to be extremely intoxicated. The man also had three active warrants for his arrest. He attempted to run from the deputy, but fell into a barbed wire fence. The man was then taken to jail.

2:07 a.m.: Deputies stopped a vehicle at a Custer convenience store. The driver ran from the area on foot, probably due to outstanding warrants on him. Several passengers were cited for alcohol-related offenses, including open containers and minor consumption of alcohol. The driver's day will no doubt come, sooner or later.

12:03 a.m.: An intoxicated man called to report that rowdy people were on their way to his residence in Hermosa to have a party. The man did not want to host such a gathering, and requested a deputy be ready to break it up. As there were no further calls, it was believed the rowdy revelers recanted their request.

12:07 a.m.: Mailbox abuse was reported near a residence on Wapiti Road, near Highway 79. An alert citizen identified the box-smashers' vehicle and deputies decided to wait for the vehicle to pass them on Highway 16A, on the way back to the suspects' home. Surprisingly, they waited but a few seconds before the vehicle passed them. A quick traffic stop and some investigation later, the deputies had one man in custody for DUI and a juvenile detained for consuming alcohol. Other charges may be pending on the drinking duo.

11:54 p.m.: A suspicious person was reportedly trying to open the doors of several downtown Custer businesses. Deputies tracked down the man, and questioned him about his activities. No damage or opened doors were found in the area. The man claimed he was "abandoned" by his friends while driving through Custer as part of a fraternity prank. After some time, the man's friends arrived to pick him up and take him home. Alcohol may have played a factor in the incident.

1:37 a.m.: A deputy stopped a vehicle on Highway 16, north of Custer, for speeding. After some investigation, he arrested the driver, a 25-year-old Hill City woman, for driving under the influence of alcohol. The driver told the deputy that she had been assaulted by her 30-year-old boyfriend earlier in the evening. Meanwhile, on Montgomery Street, an inebriated man was reportedly banging on the door of a residence, trying to gain entry. Other deputies arrived to arrest him for this disorderly conduct. Coincidentally, the man turned out to be the mysterious and allegedly assault-prone boyfriend, also from Hill City. Various charges are pending on the hapless couple.

12:03 a.m.: A deputy stopped to check on a man who had a bicycle wreck near a West Custer tourist attraction. The man was apparently not hurt, but several of the cans of beer in the case he was carrying were fatally injured. It is not known if alcohol contributed to the accident.

12:45 a.m.: Reports were received of an intoxicated man verbally abusing people and generally "acting the fool" at a semi-popular Custer convenience store. Deputies arrived and promptly arrested the 21-year-old transient for disorderly conduct.

7:01 p.m.: Deputies responded to a report of a drunk and belligerent man causing problems at a residence on Paradise Road, west of Hermosa. They stopped the man as he was leaving the residence in a vehicle. After some investigation, they arrested the 53-year-old Custer man for third-offense, felony DUI. The man had been arrested on the same charge just over a week before, at the same residence. So, same time next week?

2:50 a.m.: A man was reportedly lying in the middle of Sylvan Lake Road. A passerby stopped to help the man, who appeared to be extremely intoxicated. When the passerby told the man that deputies were on the way, the man reportedly said "I'm out of here!", and then quickly left the area on foot. The intoxicated man was not found.

11:18 p.m.: Deputies responded to a wild brawl involving at least eight people in the middle of Sylvan Lake Road, near the turnoff to the lake. Apparently various members of a wedding party had decided to take their grievances out on each other. After some investigation by deputies and other assisting agencies, one person was arrested for DUI. Several others face additional charges in the booze-fueled melee.

5:52 p.m.: A minor two-vehicle accident was reported on Mount Rushmore Road, in Custer. One vehicle apparently rear-ended the other while it was stopped to let pedestrians cross the street at a marked crosswalk. After some investigation, a deputy arrested the rear-ender for driving under the influence of alcohol.

11:51 p.m.: Deputies were called to a downtown Custer tavern to educate some patrons on the law restricting open drinks outside the licensed premises. The patrons in question learned quickly without the deputies resorting to other means.

10:49 p.m.: Thievery of malt liquor was reported at a semi-popular Custer convenience store. Deputies went there, but did not find the "forty" filcher.

1:19 a.m.: Unruly drinkers reportedly tore the toilet out of the floor at a downtown Custer tavern. The incident is under investigation, and charges may be pending.

8:09 p.m.: Deputies investigated a possible stabbing incident at a downtown Custer tavern. When everything was said and done, the "stabbing" injury turned out to have been caused by the victim falling down and hurting himself while intoxicated.

11:21 p.m.: Deputies investigated a case of possible intimidation in downtown Custer involving a prior assault and some threatening telephone calls. The deputies listened in while another call came in to the reporting person's cell phone. The suspect threatened the other man and challenged him to meet at a local convenience store to fight. Deputies went there and arrested an intoxicated (and surprised) 29-year-old Hill City man. Charges are pending on others connected to this strange and puzzling saga.

7:28 a.m.: Someone left a small quantity of their blood in an alley in downtown Custer. It is not known why or how the probably involuntary and likely alcohol-induced blood donation took place.

***

A Wild Night in Custer:

12:00 a.m.: Deputies responded to Winchester Apartments, in Custer, for a report of a drunken man brandishing a knife and screaming in the upstairs hallway. Once they arrived, they confronted the man, who was holding two large kitchen knives. He refused to drop them at gunpoint, and the deputies were forced to use a TASER device to subdue the heavily intoxicated man. Deputies then took the 27-year-old Custer man to the hospital for an evaluation.

2:10 a.m.: A passerby reported that a man was in the middle of the street, yelling and screaming, in front of Harney Street Apartments, in Custer. Deputies arrived, and found the man, who promptly ran from them. He was found a short distance away and placed in custody. The heavily intoxicated 25-year-old Custer man was verbally abusive and obstructive to the deputies. He hit his own head on the hood of a patrol car and resisted being put in the back of a vehicle. Deputies used a TASER to gain compliance from the man. He continued to hit his head on the inside of the patrol vehicle as he was taken to jail and also defecated in his pants along the way. He was charged with a variety of offenses and his head hurts a lot.

***

7:56 p.m.: A fight was reported at the volleyball courts on Washington Street, in Custer. A deputy went there and found two bloodied men who claimed they were "sparring" with each other. The two aspiring (and drunk) Rocky Balboas were told to take their training elsewhere.

9:37 p.m.: Two intoxicated men reportedly escaped a downtown Custer tavern with open alcohol containers. One man was last seen vomiting into a trash can, as he left the area. A deputy looked for, but did not find the inebriated pair.

10:01 p.m.: Deputies assisted the Highway Patrol with a sobriety checkpoint in Custer, near the junction of Mount Rushmore Road and Highway 385. No arrests were made for drunken driving, but a fair number of people reportedly chose to leave a nearby tavern on foot, rather than take their chances with the checkpoint.

10:21 p.m.: A deputy stopped a driver in the parking lot of a semi-popular Custer convenience store, for attempting to avoid the sobriety checkpoint nearby. The deputy eventually arrested the 23-year-old Custer man for a probation violation.

12:00 p.m.: A deputy and a Highway Patrol trooper dealt with three intoxicated transients that were wandering around in traffic just east of Hermosa, on Highway 40. Two of the men were drunk enough to earn a trip to the Detox facility in Rapid City.

10:47 p.m.: An underage person was reportedly trying to buy alcohol at a downtown Custer tavern. When the bartender told them to leave, they got nasty and caused a disturbance. The haughty hooligan made good their escape before deputies arrived.

10:03 p.m.: Deputies went to a downtown Custer bar for a report of an unruly customer. The person had apparently thrown their drink at the bartender, gone outside to collect some snow, and then returned to hurl a snowball at them. The snowball-thrower then escaped and has not been seen since.

5:33 p.m.: A deputy removed an unwanted person from the Custer liquor store. The person was apparently already very intoxicated, but wanted more booze. He didn't get it.

***

3:23 a.m.: Recipe for disaster: Take one Ford Explorer; add five intoxicated Rapid City men, a spotlight, and firearms. Combine with more alcohol and stir. Deputies from two counties, Highway Patrol troopers, and medical personnel sorted out the result of this stupefying mixture, which yielded a catastrophic one-vehicle rollover just south of Creston, in the far northeast corner of the county. Two of the five occupants were transported to the hospital for their injuries. The driver was charged with driving under the influence of alcohol. The other occupants all have charges pending, including open container charges and game violations. At least one dead deer was found near the crash site at the end of a trail of unopened beer cans, apparently shot by someone in the vehicle. The investigation continues.

***

9:33 a.m.: Reports came in of several people standing by a stopped car, throwing beer cans and waving a tire iron at passing cars on Highway 40, east of Hermosa. A deputy went there, but found only an abandoned and heavily damaged vehicle, which he towed. This was not the end of the story.

1:09 p.m.: A deputy assisted the Shannon County Sheriff with

THE CUSTER COUNTY SHERIFF'S LOG

a prisoner he had just arrested in Red Shirt for assault. The arrestee, a heavily intoxicated 49-year-old Rapid City man, appeared to be the same person who was hurling objects at passing cars on Highway 40 a few hours earlier.

***

11:44 p.m.: A possible assault was reported at a downtown Custer tavern. After speaking with everyone involved, the original reporting person recanted their tale of woe, and decided that nothing wrong had happened. Alcohol was a large factor in the whole incident.

2:33 a.m.: Reports were received of people running and fighting with each other in the hallways at Laughing Water Apartments, in Custer. Deputies arrived in the area, finding only blood droplets on the floor. After some investigation, two of the bloodied participants in the mini-battle were located. Both declined to press charges in the incident. It was apparently brought on by some kind of failure to communicate. And liquor.

11:00 p.m.: Deputies responded to a noise complaint at a trailer on Canal Street, in Custer. When they arrived, they detained numerous underage drinkers. Many were cited for their underage alcohol consumption, and one unlucky adult was arrested on the charge of providing the alcohol. Ah, springtime. Can summer be far away?

11:38 p.m.: Someone called to report a hitchhiker causing traffic problems on North Fifth Street, in Custer. A deputy went there and spoke with the hitchhiker, a 54-year-old Hill City woman, who told him she needed a ride. Unfortunately for the woman, she was also on parole and intoxicated. The deputy gave her a ride- to jail.

4:08 a.m.: Deputies went the usual area on Canal Street, in

Custer, for a report of a drunken man who attempted to fight with some party-goers there. The man apparently suffered some injuries during this activity. He was eventually transported to Custer Regional Hospital, and then back to Wyoming, where he came from.

10:41 a.m.: People were reportedly yelling at passing cars in front of Laughing Water Apartments, in Custer. A deputy went there and spoke with three adults who should know better about their behavior. The beer on their breath may have had something to do with their lapse in judgment.

5:08 a.m.: A drunken man brandishing a small-caliber revolver kicked in an apartment door at Laughing Water Apartments, in Custer. The tenants there apparently disarmed him and he threatened to return with heavier hardware. Deputies found the man hiding in a residence on Harbach Lane, and arrested him for aggravated assault, and other charges.

12:36 a.m.: Juveniles were reportedly yelling and breaking bottles on the Mickelson Trail, near Custer's east end. Deputies found the loud juveniles, and after some investigation, detained two of the little loud mouths for underage alcohol consumption.

3:06 a.m.: Deputies responded to a trailer park on Needles View Place. When they arrived, they found a drunk and belligerent man lying on the ground, already handcuffed. Apparently, some kind of scuffle had taken place at a trailer there, and one person had subdued and restrained the apparent suspect, a 32-year-old Custer man. The suspect was arrested on several charges.

7:25 p.m.: A deputy ejected an unruly and unwanted person from a casino in the Custer area. The man had apparently become angry when asked by the bartender to prove his age by showing ID.

***

3:31 a.m.: A deputy dealt with an intoxicated man at a Custer State Park campground. The man initially reported several different things, but he was mostly trying to get a ride to Rapid City. He did not get it.

6:24 a.m.: The intoxicated man was at it again, this time in the Playhouse Road area. He stole a bicycle from a residence, and then abandoned it in the road ditch a short distance away. The man then disappeared from the area, as he probably realized his hoped-for ride to Rapid City was going to end at a large concrete building with narrow little windows, at 300 Kansas City Street.

***

11:05 p.m.: As the old saying goes: "The squeaky wheel gets the grease". Deputies responded to a noise complaint from a recurring problem residence on Canal Street, in Custer. Their arrival broke up a juvenile drinking party, with the usual results- citations issued for underage consumption of alcohol, and at least one person who fled the scene on foot. The fleet-footed escapee was found later in a different part of town, slowed down by a broken ankle he suffered while on the run.

8:54 p.m.: A deputy assisted the Hermosa Marshal with an unruly cowboy at a Hermosa bar. The intoxicated man was refusing to leave, but eventually smartened up and accepted a ride home from a friend, rather than a ride with the deputy, to jail.

8:18 p.m.: Responding to a report from Custer Regional Hospital, a deputy went to the emergency room there to discover a car had been driven onto the lawn outside. The driver was inside seeking medical treatment. After some investigation, the deputy charged the 55-year-old man with driving under the influence of alcohol.

9:29 p.m.: Deputies assisted Pennington County units with the search for a carload of beer thieves who boot-jacked some brewskis from a convenience store in Hill City. The boozing bandits barely made it to the county line before they were overtaken by the law.

5:30 a.m.: Confused 911 calls were received from a man who said he was locked in a garage and couldn't get out. Eventually, with the help of modern GPS technology, the calls were traced to a residence on Highway 40, where a disoriented (and intoxicated) man had somehow gotten himself locked in a stranger's garage. The man was taken to the Detox. Center in Rapid City, to dry out.

9:12 p.m.: Deputies checked on a possibly intoxicated man who had fallen down a few times in front of Custer Middle School. The man claimed he was not intoxicated, but had fallen while trying to escape a mysterious white dog that was chasing him. The man declined any assistance and made it to his apartment a short distance away. The white dog escaped and has not been seen since.

8:48 a.m.: A 23-year-old Custer man decided to violate the 24/7 Sobriety Program in a spectacular but pointless way. After failing an alcohol breath test at the Sheriff's Office, the determined drinker fled on foot. He was snatched up by deputies just a few minutes later and taken to jail, anyway.

4:36 a.m.: A fight was reported at Laughing Water Apartments, in Custer. A deputy arrived and found no fight had taken place. No charges were brought against anyone at the apartment, despite one person's assertion that "The Man" was not being fair with them. Heavy alcohol consumption played a factor in this case.

5:54 p.m.: Deputies received a report of a vehicle accident and a disoriented person wandering around on Highway 89, south of Pringle. A deputy went to the area, but found only vehicle parts on the roadway and a badly damaged guardrail. While he was examining these, a severely damaged vehicle drove by him.

It turned out to be the driver involved in the accident, who was apparently very much disoriented, as he had driven the wrong way, thought better of it and turned around. The driver, a 45-year-old Custer man, was subsequently arrested for DUI and having an open alcohol container in a vehicle.

***

12:15 a.m.: Deputies stopped a vehicle on North Tenth Street, in Custer for a traffic violation. The vehicle turned out to have plates that did not belong on it. Deputies confiscated the plates. One of the vehicles' occupants did not have a driver's license. The passenger was intoxicated. Deputies would see them again.

1:49 p.m.: It was a case of bad news and worse news: the passenger from the car with the bogus license plates from the previous night showed up at the Sheriff's Office in Custer, wanting his plates back. The bad news? He didn't get the plates back. The worse news? Deputies arrested the 50-year-old Rapid City man, because he drove to the Sheriff's Office while still intoxicated.

***

7:05 p.m.: Deputies checked on a possible domestic dispute in a car at the Custer Liquor Store. No assault had taken place, but one person involved, a 54-year-old Custer man, basically talked himself into a trip to jail. Due to his belligerent actions and words, he was charged with disorderly conduct.

7:45 p.m.: Deputies ejected a man from a bed-and-breakfast establishment east of Custer, after he was reportedly drunk and disorderly there. The man accepted a ride from the deputies to an area motel, after being warned that further problems with him would result in his lodging in a much less comfortable place.

9:19 a.m.: For the second time in a week, a 32-year-old Rapid City man was detained for a violation of the 24/7 Sobriety Program, at the Sheriff's Office in Custer. It's back to the old hoosegow for him.

9:19 p.m.: A deputy came upon a vehicle in the ditch just off Highway 40, near Hermosa. No injuries were reported at the scene. After some investigation, it was found the driver had been drinking and had accidentally locked his keys in the vehicle. The driver was tested and found to be under the legal limit. However, his license was suspended and he had no insurance. He was ticketed appropriately.

7:26 p.m.: Why does the drunk cross the road? If he's in Custer, then it's to cross Mount Rushmore Road, almost get run over by a passing motorist and then disappear without a trace before a deputy gets there.

12:19 a.m.: Drunken hi-jinks near a downtown Custer tavern culminated with a 22-year-old Newcastle, Wyoming man putting his fist through a plate glass window in the front office of this newspaper. The man left the scene, but deputies tracked him like a wounded animal, by the trail of blood he left behind. The man faces some charges and his hand probably hurts a lot.

12:57 a.m.: Deputies arrested a 28-year-old Custer woman for Fourth Offense Felony DUI, after a traffic stop in downtown Custer. The woman was uncooperative, belligerent and called the deputies many names that can't be printed in a family paper.

2:01 a.m.: A deputy stopped a man riding a four-wheeler, at Eighth and Gordon Streets in Custer. At first, the deputy just wanted to speak with the man about failing to stop at a stop sign. Soon, he found the 43-year-old Indiana man had active warrants for his arrest. After more investigation, the deputy also charged the man with driving under the influence of alcohol. The moral of this story should be obvious.

2:27 a.m.: Deputies patrolling on Highway 16A, near the East Gate of Custer State Park watched a slow-moving vehicle bounce off a curb in front of them. After some investigation, they arrested the driver, a 60-year-old Rapid City woman, for DUI.

9:56 p.m.: Deputies were called to deal with a heavily intoxicated person in front of a residence on Sherman Street, in Custer. After arriving, they found the person in question to be suffering from a case of frostbite to one of their extremities. The person was transported to the hospital by ambulance.

9:28 p.m.: Deputies went to Trail View Apartments to check on complaints of noise and possible underage drinking. Several people in the second-floor apartment were given tickets for minor consumption of alcohol. One 19-year-old Custer man briefly escaped out a back balcony door. Soon, a deputy spotted someone crouching in a pile of snow on the roof. Guessing that it wasn't Santa Claus looking for a chimney, the deputies quickly arrested the man for probation and 24/7 program violations. Charges may be pending on the adult provider of the alcohol.

8:53 a.m.: Deputies detained a 27-year-old Custer man for a bond condition violation (consuming alcohol), at the Sheriff's Office, in Custer. During the arrest the man became angry, apparently because his "civil right to drink" was being violated. He went to jail, anyway.

***)

6:41 p.m.: A deputy transported a person from Custer Regional Hospital, to Rapid City Regional Hospital, for a mental evaluation.

7:23 p.m.: A drunken man was reportedly lying on the sidewalk in front of a downtown Custer business. A deputy went there and transported the heavily intoxicated 21-year-old to the Detoxification Center in Rapid City. Later, a "friend of a friend" called in to check on the man, who had apparently been abandoned on the sidewalk by another so-called "friend".

8:51 p.m.: Deputies detained a 23-year-old Custer man for a 24/7 Sobriety Program violation and later transported him to jail in Rapid City, completing the night's "trifecta of transports".

***

1:42 p.m.: Personal items were found in a front yard on Seventh Street, in Custer. The stuff was eventually returned to the owner, who apparently lost track of it while walking home half in the bag, the night before.

11:58 p.m.: A deputy gave two intoxicated Swiss tourists a ride back to their motel, after finding them arguing with each other in a downtown Custer alley. Apparently, Swiss neutrality only goes so far.

10:31 p.m.: Deputies dealt with a verbal argument behind a downtown Custer bar. They transported one intoxicated 43-year-old man to the Sheriff's Office, where he was picked up by his employer. This is probably not the best time to ask about that Christmas bonus.

10:42 p.m.: Deputies returned to the downtown bar, as they observed a 60-year-old Custer man there, who they knew was on the 24/7 Sobriety Program. The man claimed to be drinking only non-alcoholic beer, but one quick breath test later, he was in the back of a patrol car and on his way to jail.

11:42 p.m.: A deputy responding to a report of a loud party in the Aspen Road area saw a car leaving the area at nearly twice the speed limit. When the deputy gave chase, the driver lost control of his vehicle and slid into the ditch. After some struggling and a lot of bad noise, the driver was placed under arrest for DUI and possession of marijuana.

***

7:13 p.m.: Two intoxicated males were reported on Mount Rushmore Road, in Custer. They apparently staggered away before a deputy got there, but would be heard from again...

10:17 p.m.: The two intoxicated males from the earlier call appeared at a local business on Mount Rushmore Road and urinated on the floor. The two disgusting drunken dudes were detained by deputies for detoxification.

***

3:15 a.m.: An intoxicated 26-year-old Custer male came to the Sheriff's Office, in Custer, demanding to be "taken in". A deputy obliged him, transporting "Otis" to the Detoxification Center in Rapid City.

11:19 p.m.: Deputies checked on another suspicious person, at a Custer convenience store, on North Fifth Street. The 25-year-old Custer male was found to be intoxicated and unable to care for himself, so he was transported to the Detoxification Center in Rapid City. However, once there, the male began "freaking out", so he was taken to the hospital emergency room for a mental evaluation. The hospital didn't want to keep him either, so it was back to Detox, where he belonged. Wouldn't it be nice to pick and choose "clients" like all these facilities do?

3:13 p.m.: Harassing phone calls of the "drunk, dumb, and calling the wrong number" variety were received on Harbach Lane, in Custer. The caller was told to smarten up or face charges.

6: THE PRINGLE COWS AND OTHER CRAZY CRITTERS

It all started, very innocently, on a frosty Tuesday morning:

TUESDAY, FEBRUARY 22, 2005

6:44 a.m.: Cows were reported out of their pasture, on Highway 385, near Pringle. The owner was contacted to corral them.

Over the following decade, the herd of boorish bovines that I later dubbed "The Pringle Cows", from their location near the eponymous town, would appear in the column scores of times, due to their near-miraculous ability to escape thorough a fence. Their meanderings and moseyings caused lots of mirth and unfortunately, several traffic collisions.

The Pringle Cows weren't alone in causing county critter chaos. A wide variety of other animals got their own entries in the Log over the years.

1:43 a.m.: A suspicious vehicle was reported on Sylvan Lake Road. Deputies stopped the vehicle, and talked to the occupants, who claimed they were studying "flying squirrels". Rocky and Bullwinkle were unavailable for comment.

10:22 a.m.: A deputy responded to a burglar alarm at a residence on Rock Chimney Road. When the deputy arrived, he found the alarm was set off by a large woodchuck. With the help of the animal control officer, the woodchuck was evicted from the residence.

8:41 a.m.: A 911 hang-up call was received from a residence in the Custer Limestone area. A deputy found the call to have been caused by a cat jumping on the telephone's emergency button. The cat was admonished for its behavior.

5:45 p.m.: A deputy checked on a wounded deer, just east of Custer. A nearby landowner arrived and implored deputies not to shoot the deer. The landowner said it would take the deer to a vet. Game, Fish, and Parks was contacted to speak with the landowner. The deer's current condition is unknown.

9:37 p.m.: The Pringle cows went A.W.O.L. from their pasture, again. Their owner rounded them up, again.

5:02 a.m.: A non-injury vehicle accident was reported in Wind Cave National Park. A vehicle struck a buffalo, then sustained serious damage after the buffalo decided to strike the vehicle back.

2:04 p.m.: The Pringle cows were at it again, escaping from their pasture to cause havoc on Highway 89. The owners were contacted to round them up.

10:26 p.m.: A stray dog reportedly bit a woman at a residence on Spruce Street, in Fairburn. The woman then trapped the dog in a bedroom. Deputies went there and attempted to play the Dog Whisperer by winning the pooch's confidence, but were not successful. They eventually had to hook the dog with a capture pole and wrestle it into a cage. The suspect dog put up quite a fight, but was eventually captured and then transported to the 'pound in Custer, to be quarantined. The bite victim suffered minor injuries to her hand and a lecture about not taking in stray dogs.

7:46 a.m.: The usual cows were out of their pasture in the usual place, near Pringle, and the usual person was called to put them back where they usually are.

7:35 a.m.: Everyone's favorite wandering cows were on the loose again, near Pringle. The owners were contacted to pick up their wayward bovines.

1:50 p.m.: A car versus deer versus tree accident was reported somewhere outside of Custer. The car was heavily damaged, but no human injuries were reported. No word was received of injuries to the deer or tree.

6:36 p.m.: A "hazardous" deer carcass was reportedly laying in the middle of Highway 36, near Hermosa. A deputy dragged it from the roadway.

5:34 p.m.: A deputy, checking for a wounded deer on Highway 385, south of Custer, had a close encounter with a mountain lion in the road ditch. Both deputy and lion went their separate ways without further incident.

6:09 p.m.: Near a trailer park on Highway 16, a woman called to report that she was attacked by a turkey when she got out of her car in front of her residence. The woman made it inside but dispatchers reported that they could hear the turkey gobbling madly in the background as it continued to circle her house. A Game, Fish and Parks officer arrived and sent the jive turkey back where it belonged. Further turkey troubles may result in an early Thanksgiving for someone.

6:28 a.m.: The Pringle cows were up to their usual tricks, on Highway 89. The owner was contacted to pick them up.

7:19 p.m.: Reports were received of someone beating a horse behind a Custer restaurant. Deputies checked, and found the matter to be a misunderstanding involving a sick horse that was about to pass out.

9:00 p.m.: A deputy added "Raccoon Whisperer" to his list of jobs, at a downtown Custer business. Unwary tourists let a cell phone stray into the clutches of a caged critter there, whose reach turned out to be a lot longer than they thought. The deputy eventually repossessed the scratched and chewed phone from the little beast and returned it to its grateful owners.

11:15 p.m.: Deer are apparently attacking cars in pairs now. A vehicle collided with two deer on Highway 16, near the Dewey Road. One deer was DRT (Dead Right There), while the other apparently escaped.

10:12 p.m.: Another wandering horse was reported out of its pasture on Highway 16, west of Custer. The horse apparently thought the grass was greener elsewhere.

5:03 p.m.: A tenant at Laughing Water Apartments, in Custer, reported a rattlesnake outside their door. A deputy found the snake not to be a rattler, after all.

8:13 a.m.: After a long hiatus, "An entire herd of cows" was reported out of their pasture, at the usual spot on Highway 89, south of Pringle. The owner was contacted to corral the herd.

8:27 a.m.: Someone was reportedly riding a horse on the sidewalk, in front of the Old Courthouse Museum, in downtown Custer. The rogue rider was reminded that the sidewalks in Custer are off-limits to horse traffic.

2:03 p.m.: A Custer State Park ranger assisted a mare with delivering a foal, near Highway 16A, just east of Custer. Apparently the new mother and baby are doing fine.

***

10:38 p.m.: A dog reportedly escaped from a Fairburn residence, and the owner was concerned that "someone might shoot it, or the wolves might get it". The dog apparently returned home some time during the night.

7:44 a.m.: The Fairburn resident from the previous night's call reported that someone had shot at her dog, but they missed it. It is not known who shot at the dog.

***

12:04 p.m.: After a long sabbatical, the infamous wandering Pringle cows appeared by the side of Highway 89. Their owner was contacted to steer them back where they belonged.

8:57 p.m.: A deer reportedly attacked a car, near Crazy Horse, on Highway 16. Minor damage was done to the car. The delinquent deer apparently escaped the area on hoof.

9:29 p.m.: Another deer paid the price for failing to look both ways before it crossed Highway 16A, just east of Custer. Heavy damage was also done to the vehicle.

12:12 p.m.: The "hidden fence" on Highway 79 conned another person into reporting cows out of their pasture. The report was unfounded.

8:14 p.m.: A deer with an injured leg was reported on Gordon Street, in Custer. Deputies checked the area, but "Tripod" had already escaped.

12:02 a.m.: A deputy responded to a car versus deer accident on Highway 385, near the Fall River County line. Minor damage was done to the vehicle. A deputy dragged the dead deer off the highway, as the driver didn't want to touch it, because it was "icky".

8:38 a.m.: A deer caused an accident on Pass Creek Road, when it ran in front of a car. The driver swerved to miss the deer and hit a fence instead. The hoofed hooligan escaped the scene.

7:02 a.m.: A wounded deer was reported on Highway 16, near the west side of Custer. A deputy went there and found the deer to be stunned but still mobile. It promptly took off for the high timber.

6:43 p.m.: Wandering cows were reported on Carroll Creek Road.

The owner was contacted to moo-ve them.

1:33 a.m.: Deputies went to Winchester Apartments, in Custer, to investigate strange animal noises coming from behind a refrigerator there. After some investigation, deputies detained a hooligan hamster hiding behind the refrigerator. The hamster was released to its owner.

9:26 a.m.: A possible mountain lion cub was reported in a yard on Canal Street, in Custer. Deputies searched the area, but found only a lone house cat skulking around.

9:23 p.m.: A deer attacked a deputy's patrol car, on Highway 36, near Hermosa. The deputy was forced to put the wounded animal out of its misery. No human injuries but pride were reported.

1:04 a.m.: A deputy assisted fire fighters with a house full of smoke, on Wittrock Road. The smoke was apparently caused by a smoldering cat in a furnace duct, which also accounted for the awful smell.

5:31 p.m.: A vehicle struck a deer on Highway 16, west of Custer. Little damage was done to the car, apparently due to the fact the deer had already been run over at least once.

11:06 p.m.: A car versus deer accident was reported, somewhere in the Custer area. It was not known what kind of damage was done to the vehicle, or the deer's fate. The whole matter is very mysterious.

11:42 a.m.: Deputies provided traffic control while a herd of cows moseyed across the highway, near Pringle.

1:44 a.m.: Noisy horses were reported near a trailer park on the west side of Custer. The owner was contacted to quiet the noisy nags.

6:37 p.m.: A deer met with a Toyota Prius in a bad way, just south of Hermosa on Highway 79, doing severe damage to the tiny hybrid car. Mother Nature can be so ungrateful!

1:40 a.m.: A deputy found a wandering dog attacking an injured deer, on Mount Rushmore Street, in Custer. The dastardly dog escaped the scene on paw, but the deer did not, as a deputy put it out of its misery.

12:05 p.m.: Someone called from Laughing Water Apartments, in Custer, to report a dead deer in the street. This apparently upset them greatly, as they were used to petting it.

6:23 p.m.: A deputy assisted Highway Patrol units at the scene of a two-animal, two-vehicle accident on Highway 79, just north of Hermosa. No human injuries were reported, but a cow and a horse suffered fatal damage in the melee.

1:33 p.m.: A chicken coop caught fire on Freeland Drive. No human injuries were reported. However, six chickens were apparently cooked, and not in a good way.

7:03 p.m.: A rogue cow was reportedly swaggering up and down Highway 79, near Fairburn, prompting numerous calls by passers-by. Several possible owners were contacted to corral it.

6:41 a.m.: A different herd of cows south of Pringle escaped from their pasture. Their owner was contacted to get the rodeo rolling.

9:02 p.m.: "A big black cow" was wandering around the traffic lanes on Highway 16, near Crazy Horse. A deputy solved the problem by cowboying the crazy critter into a corral.

1:42 a.m.: Two out-of-state bicyclists used their cell phones to call for help after being trapped by a herd of buffalo for over two hours in Wind Cave Park. A park ranger went there to rescue the bison-battered bicyclists. A deputy assisted the ranger with getting the two back into Custer so they could retrieve their car.

7:47 a.m.: Inappropriate horse contact was reported on Pleasant

Valley Road. It appeared to be a civil matter.

7:29 p.m.: Someone reported a skunk in the Canal Street area, in Custer. A deputy gave chase, but the skunk barricaded itself in a culvert. The matter was eventually referred to a conservation officer.

7:01 a.m.: "A crazy lady" was reportedly trying to drag a wounded deer off the highway, near Crazy Horse. A deputy searched the area, but found neither crazy lady nor wounded deer.

10:30 p.m.: Serious damage was done to a vehicle crossing through the deer gauntlet on Highway 16/385, near Crazy Horse. Fatal damage was done to the deer by a conservation officer who was forced to euthanize it.

6:10 p.m.: Someone called to report a mountain lion in their backyard, just off Battle Mountain Parkway. The reporting person snapped an excellent picture of the big kitty before it left the area.

6:45 p.m.: Someone called to report a deer that was limping around on an injured leg near Laughing Water Apartments, in Custer. The person wanted someone to "catch the deer and help it". The matter was referred to a conservation officer.

5:13 a.m.: Some kind of car versus animal collision was reported on Highway 79, south of Hermosa. The animal type was not given in the report, but apparently "its guts exploded all over".

11:28 p.m.: More car/deer action was reported, near a cartoon-themed tourist attraction, in Custer. Apparently, the reporting person wanted to take the wounded deer to a veterinarian, but it was eventually euthanized.

11:34 p.m.: Strange noises and scratching sounds were reported outside a residence on Pine Street, in Custer. A deputy checked the area, finding only a deer, which was released without any charges.

1:56 p.m.: Someone reported a horse running down Carroll Creek Road. After lots of drama, including a landowner who captured the horse and threatened to shoot it if no one came to pick it up, it was finally returned to its rightful owner.

10:52 a.m.: Deputies stopped traffic on Highway 79, near Fairburn while a herd of cattle was moo-ved across the road. No problems were reported with the mass mosey.

5:34 p.m.: An unknown person in a pickup truck absconded with the carcass of a freshly killed deer, at the scene of a crash just west of Custer, on Highway 16. No injuries were reported, but the deer-nappers remain at large.

1:13 a.m.: Bison versus pickup in Wind Cave Park: it was a tie. Both lost.

8:49 p.m.: A vehicle struck an unknown animal on Highway 79, near Lame Johnny Road. Moderate damage was done to the car and the beast escaped, leaving only some hair behind.

4:19 p.m.: A chicken-eating dog was reportedly stalking new prey at a residence near Argyle. The chicken rancher had detained the dog, which was turned over to the deputy. The deputy then returned the dog to its owner, along with a ticket.

5:21 p.m.: A horse named "Duke" that deputies have come to know and love from numerous break-out attempts, was reportedly wandering the ditch on Highway 16, north of Custer. A deputy checked and found Duke to be safely contained.

10:15 a.m.: Custer's favorite three-legged deer evaded a deputy again, on North Sixth Street. Though handicapped, "Tripod" appears to be holding its own, so far.

5:42 p.m.: A lame horse was reported by a passing out-of-state motorist, somewhere in the Hermosa area. A deputy searched for the stumbling steed but found nothing. Poor directions given by the reporting person hampered the effort.

8:28 p.m.: Someone called to report a shaky deer lying in the middle of Highway 16A, just east of Custer. A deputy checked the area but the trembling beast had apparently snapped out of it and left.

4:22 p.m.: A dead rat floating in a toilet bowl was reported at a residence on Chokecherry Ridge Road, near Hermosa. The rigid rodent may be part of a larger case of harassment or attempted intimidation occurring at the residence. The investigation continues.

7:50 a.m.: Someone called to report a white pickup with a dog riding in the back, near Custer Middle School. A deputy spoke with the dog owner about putting the dog inside in below-zero temperatures.

3:10 p.m.: A doe and fawn were reportedly "trapped in some wire" on Montgomery Street, in Custer. Deputies searched the area but the dippy deer duo disappeared.

9:30 p.m.: Blood soaked the concrete of Highway 79, once again. Luckily, it was only deer blood. Minor damage was done to the vehicle that hit it.

2:49 p.m.: More blacktop-bashing bulls were feeling frisky, over on Highway 16, west of Custer. A deputy assisted the owners with the round-up.

7:50 a.m.: Deputies assisted with a cattle drive across Highway 16, west of Custer. All the little dogies got along to where they needed to be, without any fuss.

1:56 a.m.: Deputies dealt with a skunk that had somehow gotten a beverage cup stuck on its head, near a downtown Custer motor lodge. Deputies dislodged the cup, and the skunk scurried off, without spraying his rescuers.

3:47 p.m.: A male called 911 to report a white bird sitting on the sidewalk, in front of a downtown Custer tavern. The male was apparently afraid the bird might attack someone, but it was taken into custody by the animal control person without any bloodshed.

5:32 p.m.: Carousing cows were reported on South Fork Road, east of Fairburn. Several possible owners were contacted to stop their gravel gallivanting.

8:26 p.m.: A Kamikaze cow crashed into the corner of a car, on Carroll Creek Road, before careening off into the darkness and disappearing. Damage to the car was minor.

6:54 a.m.: Some rare antelope versus car action was reported on Highway 16, near the Wyoming line.

9:56 p.m.: A deer that "just looks funny" was reported near a downtown Custer motel. Funny? Funny how? Deputies eyeballed the beast but found it was doing nothing but eating grass.

2:43 p.m.: An unknown (and skinned) animal carcass was found on property, just off Bear Rock Road. Some investigation showed it to be the remains of a not-so-wily coyote.

12:19 p.m.: A deer "that does not look good" was reported near a restaurant on North Fifth Street, in Custer. Perhaps a makeover would help it.

9:36 p.m.: Why did the mountain lion cross the road? To disappear from the area before deputes closed in on him, on the east side of Custer, of course.

9:44 p.m.: A mountain lion nearly collided with a car, on Mount

Rushmore Road, on the east side of Custer. The beast bounded away and disappeared.

***

9:34 p.m.: The nightly mountain lion sighting on the east side of Custer came once again. The big cat escaped this time, but its nightly routine would prove to be its undoing...

9:50 p.m.: Once again, the same mountain lion crossed Mount Rushmore Road, on the east side of Custer. Deputies had gotten an okay from the Department of Game, Fish and Parks, so the careless kitty got whacked.

***

10:55 p.m.: A complaint came in about the "damn barking dogs" in downtown Custer. Deputies located only one damn barking dog, far away from the reporting person.

5:56 p.m.: A driver stopped to avoid turkeys crossing the road, on Highway 40, west of Hermosa. He was promptly rear-ended by a motorist behind him. Luckily, no injuries were reported. The turkeys escaped the scene.

11:30 p.m.: Car met elk in a bad way, on Highway 16, near the Custer Highlands turn. Though no human injuries were reported in the wreck, the elk expired on scene. During the night, someone decided to help themselves to the dead elk's head.

8:47 a.m.: Cattle that were either "starving or thirsting to death" were reported on Highway 36, by a passing tourist. The cattle were found to be doing neither.

9:42 p.m.: A cow with "funky horns" was reported out of its pasture, on Highway 40, near Red Shirt. Some investigation showed the crazy cow was actually roaming around on the Reservation side of the Cheyenne River.

9:18 p.m.: A complicated and confusing call involving the trapping of feral cats and the subsequent theft of the cat trap was reported at everyone's favorite trailer park, just east of Custer. Can't we all just get along?

8:08 a.m.: The infamous Pringle Cows were causing trouble again, on Highway 89. A deputy and a Highway Patrol trooper helped round them up.

7:27 p.m.: A buffalo limped away from the scene, after demolishing a Ford Fusion, on Highway 385, near Wind Cave. No human injuries were reported in the mess.

7:15 a.m.: A much-abused Subaru hit another deer, on Lame Johnny Road, near Highway 79. The foul beast responsible for the wreck escaped the area, leaving only behind only hair, stuck in the grille.

12:02 a.m.: A skunk got trapped in a window well, on Tweety Bird Lane. A deputy placed a log in the well, to act as a climbing aid. This enabled the striped suspect's escape, without any stinky spraying.

3:09 p.m.: "200 black cows" were reported out of their pasture, on Riverside Road, east of Buffalo Gap. Some investigation found that the owners were conducting a cattle drive.

1:31 p.m.: An unknown suspect was trying to shoot a turkey with a pellet gun, near Valley-Hi Apartments, in Custer. Both the suspect and his Sunday dinner-to-be apparently escaped.

9:40 p.m.: A deputy rescued a dog that got stuck trying to crawl through a house window, on North Seventh Street, in Custer. The dog suffered no injuries from his adventure.

7:00 a.m.: Rogue cows broke loose from their pasture and decided to tour downtown Custer. Deputies helped the owners round up the wayward herd.

4:34 a.m.: Someone was making "stupid hyena noises" at Laughing Water Apartments, in Custer. The hyenas in question didn't want to answer their door when deputies got there.

2:14 a.m.: A deputy whacked out a wounded deer, on Highway 16, north of Crazy Horse. The deer was wounded by an unknown vehicle.

7:20 a.m.: The Pringle Cows were whooping it up, at the junction of Highways 89 and 385, near Pringle. The usual person was called to corral them.

6:47 a.m.: A dozen of the Pringle Cows decided to mosey on in to town. A deputy corralled them on Railway Avenue, and helped the owner get them back home.

3:55 p.m.: Deputies were forced to deploy pepper spray while dealing with a vicious wandering dog on North Fifth Street, in Custer. The dog wisely decided to break off its attack after getting a snout full of the spray, and was eventually detained in a trap by the animal control person.

6:37 a.m.: A car was reportedly "attacked" by a deer, on America Center Road. The status of the dastardly deer was unknown.

6:40 p.m.: A small dog was reportedly "eating something dead", on Highway 16, near Beaver Lake Road. No carrion-crunching critters were seen in the area. It's not clear what the police were supposed to do about this.

7: AWESOME ALLITERATION

Sometimes, I just couldn't help myself- the temptation to launch penetrating puns and scathing streams of synonyms starting with the same letter would overcome my rational writing instincts. It was worth it, just to watch people roll their eyes when they read something particularly egregious.

4:12 p.m.: Pushy perfume people were possibly peddling their products in the parking lot of a semi-popular Custer convenience store. The pushy peddlers were not found.

3:56 p.m.: A possible pending probation problem was investigated in the Custer area.

4:00 p.m.: Three suspicious Suburbans were seen at Stockade Lake. A deputy talked with the drivers, and found the suspicious Suburbans were scouting sites for a family reunion.

6:53 p.m.: A disoriented duck was dithering around the dumpsters at a downtown Custer convenience center. It did not appear to want to leave the parking lot very badly. Deputies drove the daffy duck down the driveway and across the street, but it returned to its old roost a few hours later. Everyone involved decided to leave it alone to see if it would find its bearings and eventually leave. It did.

6:15 p.m.: Possible pornography problems were reported in Custer. The incident is under investigation.

2:39 p.m.: A deputy fielded false 911 calls from a Custer assisted living home. The spurious summonses were supposedly sent from a soaked phone.

8:17 p.m.: One of the problem peacocks on Moss Rock Lane was apparently punctured by a projectile and pronounced to have passed. No charges are pending in this case, as the problem peacock passed away on private property.

5:09 p.m.: Deputies checked a downtown Custer Restaurant after receiving an alarm there. The bogus burglar bell was thought to be the work of employees.

6:06 p.m.: Possible poaching was reported on the shores of Stockade Lake. A deputy checked out the possible poaches, finding them to have proper permits.

11:03 a.m.: Possible mail theft was reported on Harney Street, in Custer. The identity of the parcel-poaching person is not known at this time.

3:59 p.m.: Mailbox abuse was reported on Hilsey Road. The identity of the motorized menace that mowed down the mailbox is not known.

8:55 p.m.: A trio of transients were reportedly troubling travelers by trolling for spare change in front of a Hermosa truck stop. The bums disappeared before a deputy arrived to give them the boot.

7:07 a.m.: Someone complained about a parked pickup posing a problem on the busy streets of Buffalo Gap. A deputy checked the truck, finding it not to be a traffic hazard.

1:29 p.m.: A stash of second-hand orange road cones was discovered on Beaver Creek Road. No one is quite sure how the mangled mystery markers materialized.

11:45 a.m.: Funky fakers floated a famous phone flim-flam featuring fake family- FAIL.

8:51 p.m.: Prank phone perpetrators plied their punk profession on poor people at Trail View Apartments, in Custer. Charges may be pending.

11:31 a.m.: Petulant pet peacock problems popped up on Moss Rock Lane. The foul fowl in question were apparently pets that went wild. The original owner refused to take responsibility for the plumed poultry and the problem appears to be a civil one at this time, possibly pending an experiment on the best way to season fried peacock.

8: IS THE TRUTH OUT THERE?

Lots of strange and inexplicable things go on in the Black Hills…cops get to see way more of them than the average person. Some calls seem like they came from an episode of The X-Files, *which caused me to apply the show's famous tagline to some of the weirder things that we dealt with.*

3:23 a.m.: "Something" was reportedly going on in the parking lot of a business just north of Custer. Whatever "it" was apparently made a TV go off and the lights flicker at a nearby residence. Deputies checked the area, but found nothing. Is the truth out there?

11:29 p.m.: "Weird noises" were reported at a residence on Wazi Lane, in Custer. A deputy checked the area and heard nothing but a Michael Jackson song being played inside a residence there. The truth is out there, and it's wearing one white glove.

12:04 p.m.: A mysterious trail of blood droplets was reported in downtown Custer. The trail appeared to be from the previous night, and looked to be from a bloody nose. Whose nose was bloody, or who bloodied it for them is still unknown.

6:39 p.m.: A man called the Sheriff's Office to report seeing two tornadoes in the sky, northwest of Bear Mountain. Deputies who responded to the call reported nothing but clear sky. This case will apparently remain a mystery.

2:15 a.m.: A mysterious humming noise was reported on Montgomery Street, in Custer. A deputy checked the area, but found only an electric transformer making any noise. The reporting person insisted that the noise he was hearing was different. The mystery continues. Is the truth out there?

11:45 a.m.: A suspicious person wearing camouflage was reported in the woods on Hazelrodt Cutoff. The camouflage must have started working better, as deputies did not find the person.

6:12 p.m.: Deputies and fire units responded to a report of a cabin on fire near the junction of Highway 16A and Highway 87, in Custer State Park. Instead of a fiery cabin, the responders found one that was very well-lit by electric lights. It is not known why this may have looked like a fire.

4:47 a.m.: A call was received from a stranded motorist somewhere on Highway 40, east of Hermosa. The caller's vehicle had run out of gas, and she was "afraid that Bigfoot would get her". A relative arrived and put gas in her vehicle before either deputies or Bigfoot arrived.

12:14 p.m.: An absentee homeowner called to report excessive electricity and water use at her house in Custer. Deputies checked, but found the house to be secure, and no strange activity in the area.

8:27 p.m.: Heavy breathing and footsteps were reported outside a residence on Travois Trail, near Hermosa. Deputies responded to the area, but found nothing.

12:02 a.m.: A person called in from a trailer park on Needles View Road, to report that someone was knocking on his door, and then running away. The reporting person said that he would take matters into his own hands with a hatchet if a deputy did not arrive soon. The deputy in question arrived, but found no evidence anyone had been near the house. No hatchet action was reported, either.

5:28 p.m.: A man with no pants was reportedly sitting in a pickup truck at a Hermosa convenience store. The unknown man was not found. It was not known if he ever found his pants.

THE CUSTER COUNTY SHERIFF'S LOG

8:45 p.m.: A 911 hang-up call was received from a lodge near Sylvan Lake. A deputy went there, but found the lodge quiet and deserted. The truth is out there.

3:22 p.m.: A 911 hang-up call was reported from a downtown Custer pay phone. This is normally a simple incident to resolve. Too bad the phone in question was removed about six months ago. The source of the call remains a mystery. Is the truth out there?

11:17 p.m.: A wolf was reported crossing Highway 16, near Crazy Horse. It was not seen again. Is the truth out there?

12:05 p.m.: Someone called in from Custer Limestone Road to report their vehicle had been moved forward a few feet while it was parked, and hit a tree. A deputy checked, but was unable to determine if the movement was caused by a theft attempt, or not.

3:28 a.m.: Several 911 hang-up calls were received from an address on Walnut Street, in Buffalo Gap. There was just one problem: the house there had burned down earlier in the year. Is the truth out there?

11:39 p.m.: Several calls were received from residential areas south of Custer, reporting a power outage. One caller wanted to know if the outage was the result of a terrorist attack of some kind. It was not.

3:03 p.m.: "Something strange" was reported on North Seventh Street, in Custer. It was not known at press time what "something" was, or what the responding deputy did about it. The truth is out there.

8:05 p.m.: A passing motorist reported a naked woman was standing next to a gray van, trying to flag down traffic on Highway 79, south of Fairburn. A deputy searched the area, but found no one, either clothed or unclothed.

7:22 p.m.: A naked man was reportedly trying to flag down traffic on Highway 79, just north of the Fall River County line. A deputy went there, but the mysterious miscreant managed to elude him.

11:13 p.m.: An unidentified flying object was reported in the Corral Drive area. It was described as a "floating orb at just above ground level". The reporting person was worried the object might be radioactive. A deputy went there, finding nothing but a couple of flickering street lamps. Is the truth out there?

11:28 a.m. A 911 call was received from an unknown person, in an unknown vehicle, with an unknown problem, somewhere on Highway 40, east of Hermosa. A deputy went there, but found nothing. The cause of the call remains…unknown.

12:27 p.m.: A "green army-colored" helicopter was reportedly flying low over Montgomery Street, in Custer. The person calling in the report "did not think it was right". It was not immediately clear how the reporting person was affected by the green chopper.

6:37 p.m.: A deputy sighted a man walking down Folsom Street, in Hermosa, swinging a sword. The deputy had a quiet conversation with the man and learned that he was practicing a martial art. The man was advised to move his dojo off the street, lest someone armed with more modern weapons took his swordplay the wrong way.

8:59 p.m.: Mysterious banging noises were reported outside a trailer in the Fairburn area. A deputy went there, but found no bangers. This is apparently a recurring call at the trailer in question.

12:35 p.m.: Someone called to report a mysterious wood sculpture had appeared near Harney Peak Apartments. A deputy seized the strange sculpture for safekeeping. Anyone missing something like this is encouraged to call the Sheriff's Office.

11:15 a.m.: A mysterious black helmet was found on Highway 16, north of Custer. Darth Vader had not yet called the Sheriff's Office to claim it.

1:03 p.m.: More phantom cell phone calls were received from the Highway 36 area. Again, nothing was found. Do UFOs have cell phones?

7:59 p.m.: Someone called to report a swarm of mysterious bugs had descended on their house, on Jewell Road. It is not known what the bugs were, or what the Sheriff's Office could do about them.

8:20 p.m.: A dead deer reported in the middle of Highway 385 south of Custer mysteriously disappeared before a deputy arrived. Is it a case of life after death? The truth is out there.

12:15 p.m.: A report was received of someone "pretty much butchering a deer" near the West Dam area, in Custer. A search of the area found pretty much nothing, and pretty much no one.

11:03 p.m.: A deputy assisted a Highway Patrol trooper with an abandoned and bloody pickup truck on the west side of Custer. Rather than being a case for "CSI:Custer", the deputy found it was deer blood from recent hunting trip.

***

Monday, January 18th

No case reports were logged on this day. Is it possible nothing strange, weird or interesting happened in Custer County today? Creepy.

***

11:23 p.m.: A driver struck some kind of small "mystery animal" on Sidney Park Road. Minor damage was done to the vehicle's underside. The animal was not found, but left some whitish hair behind.

1:16 a.m.: Mysterious 911 calls were received, reporting a "biker bar fight" and a shooting, supposedly in the Hermosa area. A deputy searched the area but no bikers, fights, or bars open for business were found.

9:43 a.m.: A concerned motorist from the eastern side of the state called in to report observing someone possibly "throwing a child from a bridge" on a Highway 79 road bridge. Unfortunately, the incident happened a day prior and the man could not give a specific location or narrow it down to a particular county. Nothing was found near any Highway 79 bridges, in any county.

12:24 p.m.: A possible break-in was reported at a residence on Canal Street. Nothing was taken and no clues were apparently left at the scene. The incident remains shrouded in mystery.

8:52 p.m.: Deputies searched the area around a residence on Highway 385, just north of Pringle, for a suspicious person. Nothing and no one was found. Be on the lookout for scruffy people who say they are selling meat but apparently have none.

11:40 p.m.: A passing ambulance reported a possible structure fire east of Highway 79, near Lame Johnny Road. A deputy helped fire fighters search the area but no blaze was found. The "fire" may have been the moon coming up through the trees.

3:23 p.m.: Petty thefts and strange activities were reported in a trailer on Rupp Street, in Hermosa. There are no leads or suspects in the weird goings-on there.

9:28 p.m.: A man was acting strangely at a downtown Custer motel. He was asked to leave after regaling the clerk with tales of his involvement in some kind of elaborate drug investigation, involving trash dumpsters and complicated intrigue. The man was later found and denied making any strange statements. The truth is out there.

4:38 p.m.: A car versus deer accident was reported on Highway 36, near Custer State Park. The reporting person claimed that a "tornado" had chased them into the deer's path. The reporting person did have a small dog in their car but its name was not Toto.

11:56 p.m.: "A bright flash in the sky and a glow on the ground" was seen in the Elk Mountain area, near the Wyoming border. Deputies searched the area but found nothing astronomical or paranormal. Is the truth out there?

1:27 p.m.: An abandoned and skinned steer hide was discovered near Gillette Canyon Road. The incident probably won't make the "X-Files", as the sinister skinners left very earthly tire tracks at the scene.

11:54 p.m.: A deputy spotted a couple of carloads of youths in the Hermosa Cemetery. The deputy found the youths were apparently attempting to conduct a Ouija board session in the cemetery. The spirit-seekers were asked to have their séance somewhere else.

11:56 a.m.: It was Friday the 13th in downtown Custer...and deputies crossed paths with a black cat, in a dispute over its ownership. After a whole lot of bad noise, the black cat was returned to its owner and the matter was deemed not to be a police problem. It is unknown if anyone suffered from bad luck after the encounter.

9:12 a.m.: Someone on Lynn Drive called to report strange radio sounds (someone repeating "raspberry six" on a walkie-talkie) coming from across the road. It is still a mystery who or what "raspberry six" was.

12:29 a.m.: Strange blinking lights were reported, just west of the Custer County Courthouse. The truth was out there...in the form of a city street sweeping machine working the area.

12:17 p.m.: A strange fiberglass rod fell from the sky and landed in a yard on Rose Place, near Custer. A deputy inspected it and deemed it to be from a weather balloon...isn't that what they said at Roswell? However, nothing else strange, such as alien bodies, was found in the area. Is the truth out there?

12:41 a.m.: A vehicle with no tail lights was reported on Highway 16, north of Custer. A deputy searched for it, but it had disappeared. Maybe it was one of those ghost cars.

11:58 a.m.: "Blue powdery stuff" was reported in a driveway, just off Highway 16, west of Custer. The stuff turned out to be weed killer.

12:56 p.m.: A spray-painted panda bear symbol was reported on the sidewalk, in front of the Custer County Library, in Custer. The mysterious mark-making miscreants are still at large.

5:57 p.m.: More alarm (or perhaps, ghost) problems happened at a museum on Mount Rushmore Road, in Custer.

12:26 p.m.: More alarms rang out at the same downtown Custer museum, and once again, deputies found no ghosts, poltergeists, spirits, demons, wandering souls, shadow people, aliens, leprechauns, or signs of Bigfoot- this time.

6:27 a.m.: A report was received of an unknown concave-shaped flying object that was "half the size of the courthouse", traveling at a high rate of speed between Stagg Road and Pringle. Is the truth out there?

10:33 p.m.: A man dressed in black was reportedly walking the line, on Highway 79, north of Hermosa. It is unknown if he was headed to Jackson, or not.

11:55 p.m.: Strange flashing lights were spotted in the ditch next to Highway 79, near Fairburn. A deputy discovered the lights were not caused by some paranormal phenomenon but came from a parked tractor left there by a hay-cutting crew.

9: ALL OVER THE ROAD

The proliferation of cellphones and other digital devices have enabled every driver to become a terrible tattletale. Now, instead of shaking their heads and muttering something nasty under their breath about other drivers, the average motorist can press a button and report situation unfolding on the highway in front of them to a police dispatcher...usually, in the most dramatic and hyped-up way possible.

Once in a while, the driver making the call about the terrible things the other person did is actually telling the truth, which causes a whole other bunch of problems.

5:04 p.m.: Young children were seen setting up traffic cones across Montgomery Street, in Custer. A deputy interrupted their traffic-management experiment, and made them put the cones back where they found them.

8:11 p.m.: A concerned citizen called in to report they were following a vehicle with one tail light not working, on Highway 16, west of Custer. The vehicle was not found. It was not clear why the citizen was so concerned about a missing tail light.

8:38 p.m.: A speeding vehicle that was reportedly going as fast as ten miles over the posted limit was reported on Highway 79 near Hermosa. The semi-speedy vehicle was not found.

1:07 p.m.: A stolen tractor was reported east of Buffalo Gap. It was found a short time later, a few miles down the road. Apparently, an unknown person decided to take a low-speed joy ride.

7:13 a.m.: A deputy assisted a school bus driver with an unruly student on Sidney Park road. The student wisely chose to settle down, and continue his trip in the school bus, rather than the deputy's patrol car.

3:21 a.m.: A vehicle was reportedly going north in the southbound lane, on Highway 79, near Buffalo Gap. The directionally challenged driver was not found.

8:04 a.m.: Another call was received about an abandoned vehicle in a Buffalo Gap church parking lot. The matter is being handled by the town board. All other calls should be directed to them.

10:45 a.m.: A reckless driver was reported on Highway 385, south of Custer. The driver was stopped in Fall River County and dealt with. He was reportedly very regretful.

4:39 p.m.: Reports were received of a body lying by the side of Highway 79, wrapped in plastic. After some investigation, the plastic-wrapped transient was found to be alive and well, just taking a rest.

1:42 p.m.: A reckless motorist was reported on Highway 16, north of Custer. The reckless man was apparently driving and operating a laptop computer at the same time. The reporting person apparently tried to signal the man to close the laptop, but he ignored her.

2:04 p.m.: Stolen traffic cones were reported on Stockade Lake Drive. They are bright orange, and should be pretty easy to spot.

9:59 a.m.: Deputies assisted fire units with a burning garbage truck on Carroll Creek Road. The driver was transported to the hospital to be checked out. The singed, scorched, and smelly truck was apparently a total loss.

4:17 p.m.: Tourists reportedly hit "something" on the highway, near Hell Canyon. Minimal damage was done to their vehicle, and no injuries were reported. The unknown animal or object they apparently struck was not found.

10:00 p.m.: A tree had reportedly fallen across Highway 87, north of Sylvan Lake. A deputy checked the tree, but found it not to be a traffic hazard. It is not known if it made a sound when it fell.

7:08 p.m.: Someone drove through the window of a downtown Custer restaurant. Unfortunately, it was not a drive-through restaurant. Luckily, damage was moderate, and no injuries were reported.

7:51 p.m.: Hooligans were reportedly racing around downtown Custer in a car with profanities written on it. A deputy cornered the little devils and convinced them to clean up their act, at least for a while.

4:18 p.m.: A vehicle was reportedly parked over the three-hour time limit in front of a downtown Custer business. Charges may or may not be pending in this case.

3:27 p.m.: A motorist called to report someone throwing lit cigarettes from their vehicle, on Highway 385, just south of Custer. Deputies found the foolish firebug and fined him.

2:49 p.m.: A vehicle reportedly lost some parts on Highway 16, north of Custer. Deputies checked, but could not contact the crumbling car.

11:36 a.m.: A tourist reported they lost a small boat somewhere on Sylvan Lake Road. The boat was attached to the top of their vehicle, but was somehow cast adrift. Anyone who knows where it might have washed up is encouraged to call the Sheriff's Office.

3:59 p.m.: A driver reportedly ran past a school bus with its "STOP" sign deployed, on Highway 16A, just east of Custer. The driver did stop a short time later, for a deputy who promptly wrote them a citation.

1:52 a.m.: A deputy swerved to avoid a deer on Sylvan Lake Road, and hit a rock outcropping with rear of the vehicle. Moderate damage was done to the patrol car. The deer escaped the scene on hoof.

4:31 p.m.: Someone reported a possible drunk driver on Highway 385, south of Custer. A deputy stopped the person and found them to be sober, but "a very bad driver".

5:52 p.m.: A car versus grocery store accident was reported in downtown Custer. The grocery store apparently won. At least one person was transported to the hospital, with non-life-threatening injuries.

2:01 p.m.: A deputy patrolling Highway 16 north of Custer observed a motorcycle going in excess of 100 miles per hour and passing other vehicles recklessly. The deputy turned around and attempted to stop the motorcycle, which accelerated and continued north. After a short time the deputy terminated the pursuit for safety reasons, and continued into Pennington County to meet their responding units. The deputy noticed the motorcycle was stopped on a pull-off just up the road. When the rider saw the deputy, the chase was on again for a brief time, until the deputy again called off the pursuit due to the speeds involved. Some time later, near the Highway 244 junction, the motorcyclist apparently lost control and wrecked. He was taken to the hospital with surprisingly non-life-threatening injuries. Numerous charges are pending on the 28-year-old Rapid City man in both counties. He probably should have quit while he was ahead.

3:14 p.m.: Reckless juveniles were reportedly being pulled along on their skateboards by hanging onto the back of a pickup truck, on North Fifth Street, in Custer. A deputy dealt with the brazen boarders.

7:36 p.m.: A deputy stopped a vehicle on Highway 79, near Hermosa. After some investigation, the driver was cited for possession of drug paraphernalia, speeding, no insurance, and not having a valid driver's license. Other than that, they were all right.

1:22 p.m.: A recklessly driven rental truck was reported, just east of Custer, on Highway 16A. A deputy stopped the truck, and found the driver was attempting to eat and operate the behemoth at the same time.

6:23 p.m.: Someone called in to report cars parked in a no-parking zone at Custer Middle School. The investigation continues and charges may be pending in this case. Or not.

2:44 p.m.: "A row of pickups" were reportedly parked in the street, near Custer Middle School. A deputy arrived, but found no row of pickups. It is not clear what the phantom pickups were doing to the reporting person, or where they disappeared to.

8:08 p.m.: A male hitch-hiker was reportedly jumping in front of cars on the Needles Highway, trying to get travelers to stop for him. The man was reportedly "dressed funny". Funny? Funny how? We will never know, as the responding deputy and a park ranger did not find "Mr. Happy", as they dubbed him.

1:17 p.m.: A speeding car was reported on Deer Meadow Road. The speeder had apparently stopped at one point to relieve himself in the middle of the road, as well. The wily whizzer made good his escape before deputies arrived.

3:44 p.m.: Reportedly, a red car with pink-tinted windows was playing its stereo loudly on Montgomery Street, in Custer. The car was not found, but wherever it is, it no doubt looks tacky.

4:35 p.m.: A boat being towed by a motor home on Highway 79 decided to go for a little cruise of its own. Unlike the S.S. Minnow, the ill-fated tour did not last three hours, or even three minutes. Both boat and trailer beached themselves about one hundred feet from the roadway, after slicing through a barbed wire fence. No injuries were reported in the incident.

7:21 p.m.: A deputy assisted two motorists with a deer-damaged pickup, on Highway 385, near Pringle. The damage was actually caused in another county, but the "little truck that could" made it all the way into Custer County before it just couldn't, any more.

3:25 p.m.: A deputy checked on a person slumped over the steering wheel of their car, on Highway 36, near the east entrance to Custer State Park. The person was apparently praying, rather than in any distress.

8:19 a.m.: Close-following and finger-flying was reported between motorists on Highway 16, just north of Custer. Poor descriptions and a lack of any actual crime being committed hampered the investigation.

7:37 p.m.: Someone called to report an erratically driven semi truck that was northbound on Highway 16 toward Crazy Horse. Due to the trifecta of a poor description, a large time lapse and a reporting person not willing to sign a complaint, the truck disappeared.

12:54 a.m.: A one-vehicle, non-injury accident was reported on Highway 40, east of Hermosa. Light damage was done to a pasture fence and the vehicle's paint job acquired some "South Dakota pin striping" from its trip through the barbed wire.

Thursday, December 23rd

Freezing rain and drizzle in the early morning hours, combined with fog and poor visibility set the stage for numerous vehicle crashes, smashes, collisions, collapses, mishaps, misadventures and all sorts of slippery shenanigans all over the Southern Hills. Luckily, no serious injuries were reported.

During the morning's festivities, quite a few people insisted on calling the dispatch center to complain about vehicles in the ditch here or cars parked in the road there, apparently not realizing that things were icy and ugly everywhere and it was going to take the combined efforts of deputies, state troopers, park rangers, state highway workers and city employees to get things going again, plus a whole lot of patience from everyone. Eventually, everything started moving again.

***

11:28 p.m.: A deputy assisted a Haitian immigrant with getting his car unstuck from a snowdrift, on Highway 79, near Buffalo Gap. The man did not "speaka de English too good" but was grateful for the assistance, nonetheless.

4:00 p.m.: High-speed, high school hi-jinks were reported on Highway 16A, in Custer State Park. One carload of kids was apparently directing raised middle fingers and thrown garbage at another carload. Everyone was spoken to about their attitudes and sent on their way.

3:44 a.m.: Someone called in a "suspicious" vehicle, parked on the side of America Center Road. A deputy found it to be suspiciously empty and to have a suspicious flat tire. Deputies suspect this is the reason it was abandoned there.

5:59 p.m.: A possibly overweight dump truck was reported on Beaver Creek Road. A deputy checked for the chubby carrier, but it had mysteriously disappeared.

1:51 p.m.: A car versus rock wreck was reported on Sylvan Lake Road. No human injuries were reported and no word was received of the rock's condition.

11:58 a.m.: An off-duty deputy spotted a local Custer male driving around the downtown area under a revoked license. Appropriate charges will be brought on the 18-year-old male, who does not appear to be learning very fast.

2:55 p.m.: An unknown vehicle, driven by an unknown suspect, caused damage to a parked car at a Custer discount store, before escaping. Its current location is...unknown.

6:26 p.m.: A concerned motorist called to complain that a white vehicle was attempting to hit deer crossing the road, near Crazy Horse. He was of the opinion that, "People should respect the lives of deer more and stop trying to run them over". The disrespectful deer-dogging driver apparently had poor aim, as no carcasses or other carnage were reported in the area.

1:43 p.m.: Reports of road-raging drivers came in around the Custer area. Two vehicles were apparently chasing each other hither and yon, with the fun ending in a motel parking lot with some kind of verbal confrontation. After speaking with all those involved, deputies decided to charge a 19-year-old Custer male with reckless driving.

5:53 p.m.: A speeding Toyota Prius was reported on Highway 79, near Fairburn. This report was probably unfounded, as the average Prius may not have enough power to exceed the posted speed limit.

6:03 p.m.: "A rock the size of a Volkswagen Beetle" was reportedly blocking Highway 16, in Hell Canyon. A deputy did traffic control while the rock, which was actually smaller than Das Auto but still too heavy to drag by hand, was winched clear by highway workers.

8:18 a.m.: An illegal U-turn ended in tragedy, in downtown Custer...or at least ended in a non-injury, two-car wreck.

1:41 a.m.: It was a case of the fast, the furious and the foolish. Illegal road racers were reportedly tearing up an overlook parking lot on Iron Mountain Road. A deputy arrived in the area and assisted Mount Rushmore park rangers and others in dealing with the motorized menaces. It is not known if this crew was associated with the hapless pair of drivers that wrecked two cars nearby in a single, stupefying incident a few weeks prior.

5:34 p.m.: Someone called to report a red four-wheeler had been "terrorizing" downtown Custer over the last couple of days. The rider was described as having "that weird facial hair thing". Despite his distinctive appearance, the motorized menace was not found.

12:49 p.m.: Speeding gravel trucks were reported on Highway 385, south of Custer. A deputy stationed himself there for a while and found the trucks were averaging fifty miles per hour... in a sixty-five M.P.H. zone.

11:26 a.m.: A vicious vehicle popped itself out of gear and attacked a tree, on Mann Road. Neither the tree nor any humans were seriously injured.

10:33 p.m.: A wheel fell off a car, near Valley-Hi Apartments, in Custer. No injuries were reported but the car's driver apparently caused some damage to the crippled car's bodywork by kicking it in frustration.

2:34 p.m.: An off-duty deputy observed a vehicle driving recklessly, at the junction of Clay and Buckhorn Streets, in Custer. When the deputy confronted the driver, the 15-year-old male told him that he couldn't do anything as he was not in uniform and then sped off. It will be interesting to see if the judge has the same opinion.

10:41 p.m.: A deputy cleared dropped hay off Highway 79, near Fairburn, where it had been causing consternation to the cell-phone car crowd.

5:30 p.m.: Deer met Dodge, just west of Custer, with the deer losing it all. The old Dodge suffered only a dent on top of an existing dent.

6:07 p.m.: An ambulance crew leaving the scene of a medical call on Riverside Road reported a vehicle that was following them recklessly close. A deputy was not able to safely catch up with the vehicle, but it was intercepted near Rapid City, by another agency. The driver was then arrested for driving with a revoked license and for an active warrant.

8:54 a.m.: An unlicensed driver was observed operating a vehicle at the County Courthouse. Charges will likely follow and the driver will probably wish they had parked around the corner.

11:44 p.m.: It started as a suspicious vehicle call on South Eighth Street, in Custer. Within a few minutes, the suspicious vehicle fled from a deputy and started a short pursuit, until the suspect driver eventually lost control and crashed into a swamp, just off Pony Express Lane. Deputies arrested the driver, a 24-year-old Custer man, for Third Offense DUI and other charges and also took the passenger, a 40-year-old Custer man, to jail for an active warrant. Other than that, they were all right.

11:26 p.m.: They say no one makes house calls anymore; however, the driver of a Ford Explorer decided to make one, on Bryden Drive, in Custer. When the dust settled, the Explorer was wedged firmly into the garage between the walls and a parked car, and the driver had fled on foot. The driver, a 22-year-old Custer man was picked up a short time later and charged with various things, including a suspended license and violating his probation.

5:52 p.m.: Cops spend a lot of time driving, and often find strange things on the roadways that fell off or were thrown from vehicles. Add this one to the list of dropped doo-dads: a .45-caliber Kimber pistol. Luckily, the owner soon became aware of its sudden departure, somewhere on Highway 40, near Hermosa, and called in to claim his slightly scratched sidearm.

10:34 a.m.: Someone called to report parking problems and a vehicle not using its turn signals, in downtown Custer. It is not known if charges are pending in this case, but the investigation will continue until the sinister scofflaw suspects are brought to justice!

8:38 a.m.: Someone called again, about the "suspicious" car

parked on North Fourth Street, in Custer. It was still legally parked and not really suspicious.

7:19 p.m.: A call came in of an unruly juvenile that bailed out of his parents' vehicle on Highway 79, near Lame Johnny Road, and was running around in traffic. A helpful state trooper was able to conduct some roadside family counseling before a deputy got there.

6:32 p.m.: A deputy clocked a late model Chevy Camaro at 107 miles per hour, on Highway 89, south of Pringle. A short pursuit ensued, ending with the driver in custody on a stack of charges. The 19-year-old driver will likely not be saving fifteen percent or more on his car insurance, any time soon.

11:47 a.m.: A deputy assisted cops from another county with nabbing an escaped juvenile inmate in a stolen vehicle, on Highway 40, east of Hermosa. The juvenile escapee had apparently made the mistake of stealing a vehicle equipped with a factory-installed tracking system. Oops.

12:49 p.m.: A new arrival to the county from another state called to complain about the condition of Box Canyon Road, near Hermosa. He had apparently not driven on the road before buying a house there. The matter was referred to the county road department.

7:13 a.m.: A suspicious hitch-hiker was reported on Highway 16A, just east of Custer. A deputy checked on the man and found he was neither hitch-hiking, nor suspicious.

6:11 p.m.: Deputies did traffic control for several hours on Highway 16A, after a state snowplow slid off the roadway. Eventually the hapless behemoth was winched free. Here's a helpful winter driving tip: If the snowplows are skidding off the roads, maybe you should stay home.

7:05 p.m.: An out-of-state motorist called in a "huge fire", possibly a "slash pile or a residence", east of Highway 79, near

Fairburn, without stopping to find out which. Nothing was found on fire there.

11:51 a.m.: A remote-controlled toy car was apparently causing consternation to motorists, on Highway 40, west of Hermosa. A deputy went there and sidelined the nasty little car before it could annoy anyone else.

6:42 p.m.: Someone called 911 on their cell phone to report a traffic cone sitting "right in the middle of the road"! A cop corralled the crazy cone. Whew, that was a close one!

6:29 p.m.: An erratically-driven vehicle with no headlights was reported on Highway 385, in Wind Cave Park. A deputy quickly found the light-less vehicle, and ticketed its license-less driver.

10: IT'S FOUR-TWENTY SOMEWHERE

Second only to Demon Rum, illegal drugs caused a lot of people to find themselves in situations and places they didn't plan on...like jail.

Though usage and possession of marijuana was "kinda, sorta" becoming legal in South Dakota at the time of this book's publication, it was "go-to-jail" illegal during the incidents reported in this part of the Sheriff's Log. The decriminalization of pot hasn't made its chronic abusers any smarter or less prone to end up in the newspaper.

7:21 p.m.: Suspicious customers were reported buying large quantities of cold tablets at a Custer business. The reporting person was concerned that the cold tablets might be used to make methamphetamine. The tablets sold were found not to contain the correct ingredients to do this. It is not known if the customers were aware of this.

9:54 p.m.: Fear and Loathing in Custer County (with apologies to Hunter S. Thompson): A 38-year-old Custer man was somewhere on the edge of Hell Canyon, when the beer, whiskey and ether began to take hold. Suddenly, there was a terrible screeching and roaring all around the Hyundai SUV as it scraped along a rocky cliff on the right and then lurched back over the roadway, before sailing headlong into a 40-foot deep abyss and rolling over. At the end of it all, the driver was in the hospital and facing charges for DUI, ingestion of other drugs and other miscellaneous offenses.

11:54 a.m.: A suspicious person reportedly asked a local resident where he could buy some marijuana, near a semi-popular Custer convenience store. The suspicious person was not seen again, and it is unknown if he got his weed.

9:30 p.m.: Suspicious people were reportedly buying large amounts of cold medicine at a Custer convenience store. A deputy investigated them, but found nothing illegal taking place. Maybe they all had colds.

12:52 p.m.: A bag of marijuana was found on the floor of a Hermosa convenience store. The bag was apparently dropped by a dazed doper.

Friday, April 20th

4:20 p.m.: A vehicle slid off Sylvan Lake Road, just north of Custer. The driver was uninjured, but dazed and confused. It is not known if this was from the accident or the combination of time and date.

10:48 a.m.: Reports were received of a possible drunk driver at a downtown Custer bank. While deputies were looking for the car, it reportedly struck a coffee kiosk south of town, causing minor damage. Deputies found the vehicle and stopped it. After some investigation, they arrested the driver, a 27-year-old Custer woman, for driving under the influence of drugs.

11:33 p.m.: Found narcotics from the Custer area was turned over to deputies. As usual, anyone wishing to claim their drugs should contact the Sheriff's Office.

***

1:33 a.m.: A suspicious person was reported on Highway 16, west of Custer. The vehicle left the area before a deputy arrived, but he was not gone for good.

4:33 a.m.: The suspicious person was reported again, at another location on Highway 16, west of Custer. A deputy found the vehicle, and after some investigation, arrested the driver, a 56-year-old Rapid City man, for possession of marijuana and having an open alcoholic beverage in his vehicle.

12:49 a.m.: A report was received of a possibly intoxicated man passed out at a Custer convenience store. A deputy went there and found the man slumped over a beer display. After some further investigation, he arrested the 56-year-old Rapid City man for Driving under the influence of alcohol, as he had driven his pickup to the store. Yes, it was the same 56-year-old Rapid City man that was arrested the previous morning for possession of marijuana. Some people don't know when to quit.

***

5:35 p.m.: A deputy stopped a vehicle for a traffic violation, on North Fifth Street, in Custer. After some investigation, he arrested the driver, a 36-year-old Rapid City man, for driving under the influence of alcohol, and having a suspended license. The passenger, a 29-year-old Rapid City man, was arrested for drug possession. This incident is further proof that peppermint schnapps, marijuana, and driving do not mix well.

1:16 p.m.: Drug paraphernalia was found in a downtown Custer alley. Anyone wishing to claim their stoner supplies should contact the Sheriff's Office.

1:57 p.m.: Someone got sloppy and dropped their drug paraphernalia on North Sixth Street, in Custer. Bummer.

10:31 p.m.: A bag of marijuana was found on the floor of a Hermosa convenience store. Anyone who thinks they might have dropped their weed while dazed and confused in Hermosa should contact the Sheriff's Office to claim it.

3:58 p.m.: Deputies checked on two hitch-hikers at a semi-popular Custer convenience store. The two were reportedly on their way to Sturgis for the Rally, bearing cardboard signs reading, "STURGIS PLEASE", and "WE WON'T KILL YOU". After some investigation, one of the vagabonds, a 21-year-old Florida man, was found to have a warrant from another state. This turned out to be a case of good and bad good news for him. The good news? The other state did not want to extradite him. The bad news was that deputies subsequently found a small quantity of hashish and more than half a pound of marijuana on his person and in his backpack. The unlucky hitch-hiker was arrested and charged appropriately. It is likely he will still be in South Dakota long after the Rally is over.

3:33 p.m.: Someone abandoned their marijuana on a hallway floor at Harney Street Apartments, in Custer. It is not known who dropped the pot, or why.

5:04 p.m.: Possible illicit drug use was reported at the softball fields on the west side of Custer. A deputy went there and talked with two youths, but found no evidence of anyone littering, or smoking the reefer.

1:27 a.m.: Two future rocket scientists in a car were reportedly trying to sell narcotics to a juvenile at the intersection of Eighth and Gordon Streets, in Custer. A possible identification has been made of the dopey duo, and the incident is under investigation.

3:37 p.m.: A little green bag of marijuana was discovered in the restroom at a semi-popular Custer convenience store. Somewhere, someone is without their pot. So sad.

6:17 p.m.: Someone called to report that a bag of a mysterious green, leafy substance had been deposited on their doorstep, on Harney Street, in Custer. The person believed it to be narcotics, but further investigation proved the little green bag was just full of cloves.

7:17 a.m.: A suspicious man was reportedly asking people for drugs, outside a residence on Ninth Street, in Custer. The unidentified man then disappeared inside Laughing Water

Apartments.

3:17 a.m.: A Game, Fish and Parks officer stopped a car on Sidney Park Road. Deputies assisted him with his investigation of the carload of miscreants. The results? A 28-year-old Pringle man went to jail for DUI, possession of marijuana, possession of a controlled substance and a couple of other charges. The other unlucky occupants (including one who tried to toss a bag of reefer out the window) will likely face charges, as well.

9:55 p.m.: A dirty silver van that smelled strongly of marijuana was reportedly parked outside a semi-popular Custer convenience store. The smoky stoner-mobile was not found.

2:11 p.m.: A little green bag of something that smelled like marijuana was apparently abandoned on the floor of a Custer convenience store. The dipsy doper has not been identified.

4:29 p.m.: Abandoned syringes were reported in a trash can at a semi-popular Custer convenience store. No one has claimed them yet.

5:33 p.m.: Another one bites the dust: deputies arrested a 34-year-old Custer male on felony drug charges. This brings up a question to the dope fiends and grasshoppers still out there: Are you next?

11:27 a.m.: Inhalant shoplifters were at it again, at a downtown Custer hardware store. The huffing hooligan hopheads hit the road with a quantity of computer air duster but were identified in the process. Charges are pending on a "usual suspect" or two.

11:19 a.m.: An 18-year-old Custer male who has been appearing regularly in this column stopped by the Sheriff's Office, in Custer, to pick up some civil paperwork. Other paperwork was there with his name on it: an active no-bond warrant for his arrest. While being processed, deputies found drug paraphernalia on him, resulting in more charges.

1:55 a.m.: Deputies assisted medical staff with a drug committal at a Custer hospital. One person was transported to the Detoxification Facility in Rapid City, for treatment. However, the Detox staff apparently did not want to put up with the 39-year-old Newcastle, Wyoming male, so a deputy was forced to drive back to Rapid City and transfer the man to jail.

7:21 p.m.: Deputies assisted with a medical call on Donna Street, in Hermosa. While at the residence, they smelled something... funny...kind of like...burnt marijuana. Eventually, they found not only the reefer, but other drugs and paraphernalia.

9:30 a.m.: A deputy dealt with possible marijuana possession at a Custer-area school. The "marijuana" turned out to be tobacco... of the non-wacky type.

12:26 p.m.: A bag of possible drug paraphernalia was discovered on the sidewalk, on Sixth Street, in Custer. Some investigation showed it to be gear for smoking regular old tobacco.

12:57 a.m.: They must have been dazed and confused: Two Minnesota males were stopped by a deputy after their car made two u-turns on North Fifth Street, in Custer. Some investigation found a Mason jar full of marijuana and various pipes for consuming it. The hapless pair was arrested on a several charges.

7:23 p.m.: Deputies assisted a Highway Patrol trooper with a traffic stop on Highway 385, south of Custer, near the STAR Academy West Campus. After some investigation, the trooper discovered a large quantity of marijuana and arrested the two Fort Collins, Colorado males for felony drug possession and distribution charges. With Colorado's new law allowing possession of marijuana for recreational use, the flow of reefer into Custer County from the south will probably grow.

11: Y'ALL AIN'T GONNA BELIEVE THIS

Every cop that's worked more than a few years has a head full of flabbergastingly unbelievable tales that most people wouldn't believe. Cops call them "war stories", and nearly every one starts out with something like: "There I was...", or "Y'all ain't gonna believe this..."

While they would make poor fiction, every one of these entries actually happened...or was reported to have happened.

6:18 p.m.: It started out as a complaint from another state about threatening telephone calls coming from a residence on Pleasant Valley Road. Then, an ambulance was requested there for a possible heart attack and then for a possibly suicidal person. When deputies arrived, they confronted the possibly suicidal and definitely naked 55-year-old man who ran toward them and yelled at them to shoot him. They did...with a TASER device. Deputies quickly subdued the man and an ambulance transported him to the hospital. The man faces possible criminal charges, as well as figuring out what kind of story to tell his parole officer.

8:14 p.m.: Someone called to report a person possibly hurt or lost on the Mickelson Trail, in Custer. The reporting person saw a dog she knew to belong to a regular trail hiker run past her residence, trailing a leash, but with no hiker attached. Deputies checked the trail and found the hiker some distance away, safe and sound. The dog apparently got away from her.

8:40 p.m.: Another someone called 911 to complain about a

deputy driving his vehicle on the Mickelson Trail earlier. It was quickly explained to him that the deputy was searching for a possibly lost or injured person, and that emergency service vehicles are allowed by state law to drive on the Mickelson Trail. The person was also advised to use 911 for emergency calls only. We can't make this stuff up, folks.

***

12:56 p.m.: A nine-year-old child somehow locked himself in a locker at Custer High School. Deputies went there to assist the Fire Department in freeing the trapped youth.

6:46 p.m.: Deputies responded to a residence on Pine Street, in Buffalo Gap for a report of some kind of altercation involving a man with a chainsaw that was trying to cut down a fence. Apparently the location of the fence has been under dispute for some time. After sorting it all out, no one involved wanted to press charges, so the issue will remain a civil one.

7:00 p.m.: Telephone harassment was reported at a Custer motel. The suspect was apparently looking for someone named "Ben Dover". Ben was not there. The little smart-aleck responsible was contacted by a deputy and told to stop or be prosecuted.

10:01 p.m.: Someone called to report a mountain lion was sitting in front of a residence on Pine Street, in Custer. A deputy went there and did find a lion...made of plastic. The polymer pet was not put in custody.

10:14 p.m.: Someone called to from another county to make a complaint about a federal law enforcement officer. The person was referred to the agency the officer works for. It is not known why the reporting person decided to call a county sheriff's office in another county to complain.

2:47 a.m.: Someone reported a "female in a wheelchair" passed out in front of a downtown Custer convenience mart. A deputy went there to find a man in a regular type of chair taking a nap.

The man later woke up and went about his business.

4:58 a.m.: Someone called 911 to ask for assistance in contacting a telephone operator in New Zealand. The person was advised to call directory assistance. It can be a criminal offense to misuse the 911 emergency numbers.

10:38 a.m.: A deputy dealt with a confused person who believed that she had to report for work at the Sheriff's Office. She apparently did not.

8:55 p.m.: Deputies assisted STAR Academy staff with searching for two escaped juvenile inmates, south of Custer. The two were recaptured the next afternoon, when they wandered out of the woods just a few miles away from the facility. Apparently, the two had become disoriented in the dark woods, and were frightened by what they thought were mountain lion noises.

1:32 a.m.: Deputies responded to a 911 hang-up call on Canal Street, in Custer. After much question-asking by deputies and lots of dissembling, obfuscating, and fly-specking by the people there, it was determined that a pointless verbal argument had taken place. At least one person chose to flee on foot before deputies arrived, for unknown reasons. No one felt like chasing after the person, as no crimes appeared to have been committed.

7:39 p.m.: Deputies grappled with a confusing situation in the Custer area that started out as a welfare check, and then became a possible assault, changed into a medical call, and ended up as a keep the peace call. Locations involved in the stupefying and ultimately pointless outing included a trailer park on Spring Place, Winchester Apartments, and Custer Regional Hospital.

11:15 a.m.: A domestic dispute was reported on Second Street, in Fairburn. One person involved in the dispute made the mistake of showing up angry at an off-duty deputy's house, and was briefly detained in handcuffs on the front porch swing until other deputies could sort out the mess. Eventually, the incident was found to be just another verbal dispute, and everyone was sent on their way.

10:32 p.m.: Two suspicious people were reportedly trying to break in through the back window of a downtown Custer motel. Deputies descended on the dastardly duo, only to find that they were tenants there, trying to fix the fuse box for their room.

10:28 p.m.: Two people were reportedly fighting in front of the Custer Post Office. After a deputy and the two people "had a meeting of the minds", the two were sent home with a warning.

2:51 a.m.: A person called from Rapid City to report that several Custer residents had been harassing her by pumping nerve gas into her trailer house. It is not certain what is actually going on in this case.

5:11 p.m.: Suspicious activity was reported on Lincoln Street, in Custer. The suspicious activity turned out to be a propane delivery.

9:45 a.m.: Mailbox shenanigans were reported on Granite Heights Drive, in Custer. One person was admonished not to use someone else's mailbox to mail things from.

11:05 a.m.: An off-duty deputy reported a person was trapped inside the bay of a downtown Custer carwash. The person was apparently not able to figure out how to open the automatic bay door from the inside. The person apparently found the button before another deputy arrived.

8:53 a.m.: Children were reportedly teasing a dog at a residence on Canal Street. The reporting person requested that deputies be there to guard the dog from teasing after school got out. Ummm…no?

4:06 a.m.: Concerned city workers called in breathlessly to report a suspicious vehicle that was parked on private property in downtown Custer. They were worried about the vehicle because it appeared to have exhaust fumes coming from its tailpipe for a long time. A deputy checked, only to find the exhaust fume plume to be steam from a nearby sewer grate.

2:26 p.m.: Deputies assisted fire fighters with a flurry of false fire alarms in the Custer area. One was caused by burnt breakroom popcorn, one by panicky people mistaking a legal burn pile for a structure fire, and another incident which will remain a mystery.

3:33 p.m.: A 911 call was received reporting an accident "downtown, near the Post Office". Some investigation found that the Post Office in question was actually in Hot Springs. Folks, don't assume that your randomly dialed 911 call will go to the same town you are in. Tell the nice people at the dispatch center the actual name of the street you are on and the town you are in.

7:19 p.m.: Someone called to report that an acquaintance's apartment at Trail View, in Custer, had been stripped of its furniture. The person also reported that their acquaintance was nowhere to be found and had been replaced by six to eight Mexican men. Some investigation by deputies found that the reporting person had walked into the wrong apartment.

9:12 a.m.: Someone called from Custer High School requesting that a deputy take custody of a student there who kept falling asleep in detention. This turned out to not be a law enforcement matter.

10:19 a.m.: A deputy grappled with a strange tale involving disputed hunting permission and a shotgun pellet-peppered pickup, just off Highway 36, near Custer State Park. Some investigation showed that no one was sure just where or when the truck had acquired the double-ought-sized holes in question, or whether they were connected with the hunting dispute.

2:33 p.m.: Someone called from a semi-popular Custer convenience store to report a possible drunk driver. When asked what the supposed drunk was doing, the reporting person said that she knew a drunk when she saw one. Deputies did not locate the supposed drunk.

***

Friday, December 25th, Christmas Day

11:50 a.m.: The Christmas Spirit was apparently not working for a couple of motorists who had some kind of traffic dispute, on North Fifth Street, in Custer. Both of the drivers will likely be on Santa's "naughty" list next year.

***

12:27 p.m.: Someone in a Toyota Prius apparently drove off from a Custer convenience store without paying for their gas. Despite what you may have heard from certain celebrities, even the Prius uses gasoline. The owner will be contacted to settle the bill.

7:41 a.m.: Someone called to report that driver of a truck parked across from Custer Elementary was "just staring at the playground" and he was "creeping them out". The creepy trucker turned out to be waiting for school maintenance personnel to unload a delivery from his vehicle.

11:03 a.m.: A deputy transported a juvenile delinquent from the Juvenile Services Center in Rapid City, to the airport there. As directed by a court order, the deputy put the wayward youth on a plane bound for another state. This is apparently a more modern version of giving someone a ride to the county line and telling them to start walking.

5:52 p.m.: More drama between a star-crossed couple was reported at Trail View Apartments, in Custer. This time, no intervention by law enforcement was required. They say that breaking up is hard to do.

8:02 a.m.: Harassment by text messaging was reported among some high school students in the Custer area. OMG! The matter was referred back to the school for disciplinary action.

7:03 a.m.: Calls were received about an ongoing civil matter involving child custody. The caller became belligerent with dispatchers and was eventually warned to stop calling the Sheriff's Office.

7:10 p.m.: A man reported that he had gone onto someone's property in the Custer Highlands area, to ask a question. He was confronted by an unknown male who pointed a gun at him, and told him to leave. The man did not want to press charges, and wasn't sure which residence he was at.

10:45 p.m.: An anonymous man called to report that someone was moving out of Trail View Apartments, in Custer, making too much noise. The suspected noisemaker was gone before deputies arrived. Problem solved!

1:40 a.m.: A man called from Red Valley Road, wanting to speak with a deputy about Gandhi. Strange calls are often received from this person in the early morning hours.

7:01 a.m.: Deputies scoped out a sketchy suspect hanging around a Custer hospital. Further investigation found the man not to be involved in criminal activity but in need of medical treatment...which he got.

9:21 a.m.: A volunteer fire fighter called to report a barrel was floating in French Creek, just east of Custer. The fire fighter and a representative of the Emergency Management Department responded to the scene to find...an empty barrel floating in the creek. Later, the landowner (and barrel owner) called wanting to press trespassing charges against the intrepid investigators. You can't make this stuff up.

12:21 a.m.: While working traffic enforcement in a road construction area on Vilas Street, in Hermosa, a deputy stopped and cited a Rapid City juvenile for running a stop sign, driving with a suspended license, no insurance and other violations.

The area has been the subject of several complaints about careless driving…apparently, all caused by the same person.

10:32 p.m.: A fire alarm was received from a fire fighting station on Tatanka Drive. Apparently, a fire fighter set off the fire alarm while cooking eggs. The eggs were apparently a total loss.

12:34 a.m.: A deputy stopped a strangely-driven vehicle on Highway 89, south of Pringle, to check it out. The vehicle occupants said they were lost and trying to find a house. The deputy sent them on their way with a warning, noticing that the back seat passengers were busily eating pizza from a take-out box. The deputy followed the vehicle at a distance and soon saw the very same pizza box lying in the roadway. He stopped the vehicle again and cited one of the hungry travelers for littering. Further investigation resulted in another one being cited for underage alcohol consumption. Hopefully, it was a really good pizza, considering how much it will eventually cost.

4:28 p.m.: Someone called from Hermosa to complain that a family member has been telling other people that she was stealing things. Gossip is not generally a law enforcement matter.

2:47 p.m.: Someone called to complain that women were in a Custer park, sunbathing in "indecent" swim suits. A deputy checked the area but found no one to be violating any indecency standards. This qualifies as our "you can't make this stuff up" call for the week.

9:01 p.m.: What had seven open containers, three minors drinking, three bags of marijuana, two drunk drivers, one piece of drug paraphernalia, and a stolen pistol with the serial number scratched off? It would either be part of the newest version of "The Twelve Days of Christmas", or the list of charges racked up in just two hours during a joint Highway Patrol/ Sheriff's Office sobriety checkpoint on Highway 40, east of Hermosa.

10:10 p.m.: Unidentified hooligans in a white Ford Bronco were reportedly stealing firewood from the front of a large retail store, in Custer. The white Bronco was not found. Al Cowlings and O.J. Simpson could not be reached for comment.

7:27 a.m.: Someone altered two Canal Street signs, in Custer, by painting over the "C". The little hooligans responsible have not been found. Yet.

1:14 p.m.: Someone called to report a suspicious vehicle that had been parked in front of a downtown Custer business for several days. The reporting person was concerned the car was stolen or that there might be a dead body in the trunk. Neither was true.

***

7:14 p.m.: Deputies defused a dispute between neighbors at a trailer park on Highway 16, west of Custer. They would be back.

8:13 p.m.: Deputies went to the same place and advised one person involved in the previous call to grow up and act like an adult. It remains to be seen if this advice will be heeded.

***

4:13 a.m.: The owner of a campground on Fourth Street, in Custer, called to complain about the noise from the city street sweeper. No action was taken, as no crime was committed.

1:11 a.m.: Someone called to report a noisy "hand blower" being used at a downtown Custer bank parking lot. Further investigation showed the "hand blower" was actually a street sweeper at work.

5:58 p.m.: Someone chose to call in a person that was "suspiciously digging" in a field next to Highway 385, in the Wind Cave area. The dastardly digger turned out to be a researcher working for the Park Service…wearing a Park Service uniform and driving a government truck.

5:55 a.m.: An alarm came in from a tourist attraction on Highway 16, near Cooperative Way. A deputy went there and found some damage to the building and one lone size 12 shoe. After checking the area, he located a man who appeared to have lost all his clothing but his underwear, walking alongside the highway. The intoxicated man may have been connected to the incident and is likely facing charges.

11:56 p.m.: "Knocking on doors and windows" was reported at a residence on McDermand Street, in Hermosa. Deputies descended on the area but found no knockers in the area.

12:49 p.m.: Someone called to report a man trying to impersonate a law enforcement officer, at Winchester Apartments, in Custer. The 40-year-old Hill City man was apparently not dressed for the part and had no identification to help carry out the ruse. The man was eventually located by the real cops and promptly arrested for impersonating a law enforcement officer. The man did turn out to have some connection with the legal system, though, as he was currently on probation.

***

6:20 p.m.: The third time was the charm for a heavily intoxicated 47-year-old Indiana man; after deputies ticketed him for urinating in a downtown Custer alley, investigated his irrational behavior at a local business and finally followed him to the hospital after he called an ambulance because he was out of pain medications. After being released from the hospital, the man was taken to the Detoxification Center in Rapid City.

9:57 p.m.: The 47-year-old Indiana man was dealt with by deputies a fourth time after he took a work vehicle without permission and drove it to a downtown Custer tavern. The vehicle was recovered and the man ejected from the bar. So, same time tomorrow?

***

12:40 p.m.: A man wearing a ski mask walked into a downtown Custer bank, took a look around and then left the area on a four-wheeler. Deputies found the man, who was wearing the mask because his face was cold, who said he was just looking for free calendars. Deputies lectured him about the importance of not scaring bank employees.

4:05 p.m.: A 911-hang up call was received from a residence on Renegade Pass. It was caused by a person demonstrating the 911 system to a relative. Apparently, it worked.

1:33 p.m.: A paper delivery person called to report they were worried about a downtown Custer business owner who had not picked up any papers from the front of their shop for a week. The paper person apparently neglected to notice the sign on the door announcing the business was closed for this period.

5:50 a.m.: A person was reportedly walking down the center of Highway 16, near the Custer Golf Course. When asked by the reporting person what he was doing, the man replied that he was "escaping hatred". Deputies arrived and advised the man to escape hatred somewhere else, lest he be run over.

12:14 a.m.: A well-known tenant at Valley-Hi Apartments, in Custer, called to complain that persons unknown have been tearing down notes she posted on her apartment door, and wanted a deputy to process the notes for fingerprints. Not surprisingly, this didn't happen.

***

11:46 p.m.: Deputies went to Laughing Water Apartments, in Custer, for a noise complaint. The naked and intoxicated noisemaker was told to go to sleep and be quiet. Did he listen? No.

12:30 a.m.: Deputies returned to Laughing Water Apartments

THE CUSTER COUNTY SHERIFF'S LOG

again, to deal with the still-noisy (and still-naked) man from the previous call. The man was taken to the Detoxification Center in Rapid City, after deputies got him to put some damn clothes on.

***

5:31 p.m.: The strange tale of the Mysterious Man in Black began on Highway 79 with a burst of 911 calls from the Dry Creek area. A mysterious man dressed in black was reportedly running in and out of traffic and at one point climbed into the car of a stopped motorist, then dialing Dispatch on his cell phone asking for help before disappearing again into the darkness. Deputies and Highway Patrol troopers searched the area but the mystery man had vanished.

10:25 p.m.: Mr. Mystery reappeared in the same area, attempting to flag down traffic, walking in the road and generally making a nuisance of himself. He succeeded this time in attracting the attention of a roving Highway Patrol trooper, who promptly detained the 33-year-old Rapid City man. The man claimed he was just trying to hitch a ride. He finally got a ride from a deputy...to jail.

***

12:24 p.m.: A suspicious furniture salesman was reported in downtown Custer. The sleazy seller scampered off before deputies arrived. The furniture was thought to be of the "fell off the back of the truck" type.

12:55 p.m.: Possible fraud involving misuse of someone else's name to publish a letter to the editor was reported at the Chronicle office in downtown Custer. The incident is under investigation.

2:53 a.m.: Here's a great example of why there is no such thing as a "routine" police call: A deputy went to investigate a "routine" one-car accident with no injuries, on Highway 16, near

Hell Canyon. The car turned out to contain several intoxicated people, including two juveniles. The car's driver ran from the deputy on foot, disappeared into the tall timber and was not seen until...the 21-year-old Rapid City man reportedly stole a pickup truck from in front of a semi-popular Custer convenience store. It didn't end there; the suspect was spotted near the Three Forks junction, in Pennington County by the Highway Patrol and chased to the Rapid City limits, where two of the vehicles' tires were deflated by spikes and a trooper shoved the disabled truck off the road with his vehicle. Once again, the suspect took flight on foot but to no avail. He is currently at the Pennington County Jail, with a whole heap of charges on his head. Some "routine" call, huh?

9:42 p.m.: What began as a motorist assist on Highway 40, east of Hermosa ended with a deputy seizing a set of substituted license plates and citing the driver for not having a valid license. The plate substitution was rather creative, involving expired plates from two different vehicles, with validation stickers slapped on from a third car. This is generally frowned upon.

8:11 a.m.: Someone stole the central figure from a vintage nativity scene in front of a downtown Custer motel. Thieves make the Baby Jesus cry.

11:15 p.m.: Some kind of incident involving the smearing of a bologna and mayonnaise sandwich all over someone's door was reported at Trail View Apartments, in Custer. The sneaky sandwich-smearing may have involved one of the usual suspects, who knew nothing about it.

6:40 p.m.: A misdialed 911 call was received from a residence on Second Street, in Hermosa. A deputy checked the residence and found all was well. He even received a cookie for his troubles.

1:47 p.m.: A large stack of Christian music CD's was reportedly stolen from a vehicle on Crook Street, in Custer. Perhaps the perpetrators will learn something from the spiritual songs and renounce their thieving ways.

11:53 a.m.: Dispatchers received several phone calls from a scam operation, asking for financial information and threatening "legal action" if they did not comply. It is not known why the clueless crooks continued to call a telephone number that is always recorded and goes directly to a law enforcement agency, but they were told in no uncertain terms to stop or face real legal action.

***

Monday, February 21st

Nothing apparently happened in Custer County, today. Or perhaps no one wanted to talk about it.

***

9:08 a.m.: Possible harassment was reported by some of the usual Valley-Hi Apartments people. A long, tangled tale of tenants switching each other's mailbox labels was apparently what constituted "harassment". Everyone involved was advised strongly to grow up.

9:34 a.m.: An 18-year-old male called the Sheriff's Office to complain about being ejected from a downtown Custer grocery store for suspected shoplifting. He apparently wanted some kind of legal action taken against the store. The male was given a quick education on the concepts of private property and the right to refuse service to a customer. You can't make this stuff up.

11:02 a.m.: Deputies confronted a man armed with a knife at a residence on West Montgomery Street, in Custer, while investigating a report the man was suicidal. When they drew their guns, the man made the right choice and dropped the knife but attempted to run away. One deputy then turned on his TASER device and aimed it at the person, who said, "Oh, no! Not the TASER." The man then complied with deputies instructions and was transported to Rapid City for a mental evaluation. Criminal charges may also be pending on the person.

3:51 p.m.: A trucker driving a malfunctioning vehicle requested a police escort from Custer, to Rapid City, to make sure his vehicle would get there. He was asked to find other resources to help with his troubles, as this kind of thing is usually the business of tow companies, not the Sheriff's Office.

2:58 a.m.: A paper delivery person called to report that they could not find the clerk at a convenience store on North Fifth Street, in Custer. A deputy arrived and found the clerk, who was apparently in the back room counting cookies. Or so they said.

12:13 p.m.: Someone reported the flag in front of the Custer YMCA was hanging upside-down. City workers were contacted to fix it. No kidding.

3:29 p.m.: Two well-known reporting people came to the Sheriff's Office once again, to attempt to entangle deputies in a civil child custody matter that the deputies have no jurisdiction over. After one person began cursing at the deputy, the pair was asked very nicely to leave.

7:03 a.m.: Silly food-smearing shenanigans were reported on South Tenth Street: someone who needs to get a life and/or grow up attacked a helpless car with various condiments.

9:08 a.m.: Someone called the Sheriff's Office, wanting to know if it was illegal to run on the sidewalk in front of the county library. It is not.

7:59 a.m.: Someone called 911 to breathlessly report that a car was parked on Third Street, in Custer, putting out a cloud of blue smoke "like the engine was running." Not surprisingly, the car was gone before a deputy arrived.

11:04 a.m.: A deputy investigated felony fraud involving a credit card belonging to a recently convicted and incarcerated Custer man. The fraud was likely perpetrated by some of the man's erstwhile "friends". There really is no honor among thieves.

8:52 a.m.: A 53-year-old Pringle man showed up at the Sheriff's Office for his morning's 24/7 Sobriety Program appointment. Unfortunately, he chose to drive himself there under a revoked driver's license. Deputies soon detained him for the license violation and a probation revocation.

1:51 a.m.: Deputies caught an intoxicated 31-year-old Edgemont male setting off firecrackers at the intersection of Fourth and Crook Streets, in Custer. The man's parole officer was less than amused when contacted by the deputies and asked them to find the man a nice place to stay for the night.

***

8:21 a.m.: Deputies spent some quality time sorting out a reported assault near a Custer-area alternative school. One of the participants, an 18-year-old Custer male who seems to appear in this column nearly every week, was eventually arrested for simple assault.

7:39 p.m.: Meanwhile, the people hovering on the fringes of the previous day's assault complaint did not sit idle. After much investigation, it appears that the 43-year-old mother of the 18-year-old male arrested at the Custer alternative school will be charged with felony witness tampering, in connection with the case.

***

2:34 p.m.: Someone called to report a dead sheep in a fence, on Foothills Drive, near Hermosa. It is not clear how this is a police matter, unless of course, the sheep was the victim of foul play.

8:33 a.m.: A male called from Custer, wanting deputies to "hold" from serving an arrest warrant on a relative. There are many reasons why deputies cannot "hold" arrest warrants.

7:19 p.m.: Suspicious people in a mini-van were reported on Clay Street, in Custer. A deputy rousted them and found they were neither suspicious, nor Canadian, but merely selling vacuum cleaners.

8:44 p.m.: A vagrant was reportedly mooching around a Hermosa pizza joint, looking for free food. A deputy gave the man a ride to the county line, near Hot Springs. The bum reported that the pizza he got gratis was pretty tasty.

2:59 p.m.: Plenty of peacock problems were posed by a neighbor, on Rose Place. Allegedly, the brightly-plumed pests had been defecating on another person's porch. One of the birds apparently expired on the property in question, leaving its corpse in a bad place. The whole thing turned out to be a civil problem.

9:31 p.m.: Someone brought a surly son to the Sheriff's Office, in Custer. The person wanted deputies to "do something" about the son's attitude. A deputy gave the boy some advice and counseling.

11:43 a.m.: A deputy checked on a suspicious man at a Custer medical facility who was "hitting on everybody". Unless it involves physical "hitting", this is not generally a crime.

5:10 p.m.: A concerned citizen called on his cell phone to complain that a driver gassing up a car at a Custer convenience store "looked to be about 12 years old". The citizen was apparently not concerned enough to talk with the possible underage driver himself, so a deputy completed the task. The person turned out to be old enough to drive and had a valid license.

1:11 a.m.: Two suspicious grocery bags were spotted in the Custer Post Office lobby. A deputy checked the bags, only to find they were full of...groceries, likely left for a food drive in the lobby.

6:46 a.m.: A deputy transported a prisoner from Rapid City, to Custer, for court. The 35-year-old Kansas man had just been transferred from the Meade County Jail. The prisoner was then turned over to a Fall River County deputy after his court appearance, so that he could face more charges in Hot Springs. They say it's nice to be wanted, but probably not like this.

2:03 p.m.: A deputy gave a Custer male a present for his 18th birthday; a transfer from the Juvenile Services Center in Rapid City, to the adult jail, also in Rapid City, where he continues to sit on pending felony charges.

2:59 p.m.: A recent Custer High School graduate called to complain his mother would not give him his diploma back, after he moved out of the house. This is most assuredly a civil matter.

6:11 p.m.: Someone called the Sheriff's Office wanting to know "if they were in trouble, too", as a friend had just been arrested. If you have to ask, you probably are.

7:06 p.m.: A dirty maroon car was sitting at the end of a driveway on Highway 16, near Four Mile, making the reporting person "nervous". A deputy rushed there to expose the secret of the sinister car and found...a teenage girl gabbing on her cell phone.

6:24 p.m.: A confusing 911 call sparked a lot of bad noise and blather at a trailer park on Needles View Place. When a deputy got there, it could have been a poaching complaint. No wait, maybe it was a family fight. Uh... maybe it was a neighbor dispute. Nope. After some frustrating investigation, the deputy determined nothing had really happened there that needed the attention of the cops.

1:17 a.m.: Deputies spoke with a person at the Sheriff's Office, who apparently wanted to complain about various ethnic groups in Custer. Deputies were not able to help him.

12:41 a.m.: Noisy tenants were reported at Harney Street Apartments, in Custer. When questioned by deputies, the tenants in question said the noise was caused by a tickle fight. The two ticklish tenants agreed to be quiet in the future.

3:31 p.m.: Intimidation and harassment was reported between several people in the downtown Custer area. The problems apparently started on a computer-based social networking site and deteriorated from there. Everyone involved was advised to turn off the computers…and the drama.

9:14 p.m.: A caller breathlessly reported what appeared to be a blanket-covered body, strapped to the roof of a tourists' car, in Custer. Some investigation showed the "body" was put together by pranksters recreating a scene from "National Lampoon's Vacation". It was a pretty good gag…until somebody called the cops.

10:07 p.m.: Someone zipping down Highway 16A, just east of Custer chose to call in a "suspicious" vehicle parked with no lights by the roadside. Too bad the reporting person wasn't driving a bit slower- he might have noticed some other suspicious things about the vehicle, such as the police light bar on the roof or the reflective stripes and reflective writing that said "Custer County Sheriffs' Office".

8:01 p.m.: Neighbor troubles that began with a complicated story of abandoned houses and shooting skunks climaxed in a fist fight and a flurry of threats between several people, in Buffalo Gap. Charges may be pending on everyone involved.

7:26 p.m.: Someone called 911 numerous times to report a fight. When questioned about the location, the person was only able to describe it as "Sesame Street". Some investigation found the calls did not involve Big Bird, Burt, or Ernie, nor did they come from

Custer County. Heavy alcohol consumption was apparently a factor in the calls.

3:36 p.m.: A suspicious person was reportedly sitting at the corner of Bluebell and Wildcat Streets, in Custer, and had apparently told someone he "was on a killing spree". Some investigation showed the killing spree in question to be of the electronic type, as the person had no weapons but was concealing a video game.

2:17 p.m.: Numerous road signs were reported missing on Sylvan Lake Road. So, if you see some joker with something like fifteen highway signs on the walls of his den, give us a call.

4:26 p.m.: Theft of tools was reported at a residence on Cross Road. Charges are pending on a suspect, who happens to be in custody for a stack of other felonies. Won't he be surprised?

3:36 a.m.: A deputy checked on a suspicious person in the downtown Custer area, finding a baker who was out at that ungodly hour, because…it was time to make the donuts.

12:09 p.m.: Theft of dirt was reported in the North Pole Road area. If anyone comes across it, it is likely brown in color.

11:08 a.m.: A man came to the Sheriff's office, in Custer, to complain that deputies were "watching" him. As it turned out, they weren't, but maybe they should.

***

8:01 a.m.: A man on bicycle-back was reportedly yelling at passing cars, on Highway 16A, near the Custer State Park office. Park rangers dealt with him but he would be heard from again…

5:08 p.m.: The loud-mouthed bicycle rider surfaced again, hollering "help!" near the Custer Chamber of Commerce lot. He disappeared, or perhaps rode away, before deputies arrived. He would be heard from yet again…

5:20 p.m.: ...when the hollering hooligan hurled a brick through the back window of a parked pickup truck, in a downtown Custer alley. Deputies intercepted the man east of Custer and arrested him for intentional damage to property. They also returned his "borrowed" bike to the Custer State Park resort it belonged to and then...

7:04 p.m.: ...after booking and release, a deputy gave the now bicycle-less man ride from the Sheriff's Office, to the Custer State Park Visitor's Center.

***

11:08 a.m.: Most people spent Christmas Eve and Christmas morning with their families. Someone with no life and no conscience decided it was a better use of their time to cut numerous wires on a rancher's fence, south of Fairburn. Anyone with information on the incident is encouraged to contact the Sheriff's Office.

***

1:45 a.m.: A deputy arrested a 23-year-old Hill City man for DUI, after a traffic stop on Highway 16, just north of Custer.

3:58 a.m.: The passenger from the previous DUI arrest came to the Sheriff's Office, in Custer, to bail out the driver. The 27-year-old Hot Springs man was then detained for an arrest warrant from another county. These guys should probably call it a night.

***

8:21 p.m.: Reserve deputies provided security at the Custer High School Valentine's Day dance. It is unknown if their presence deterred Cupid from firing any arrows at the attendees.

12:14 a.m.: Someone called 911 on their cell phone to report "Illegal dumping" from a sinister unmarked semi-truck, at the creek crossing on 7-11 Road! A deputy raced there to find...

a well-marked Custer County tanker truck sucking up water to spray on the dusty road.

11:25 a.m.: How not to get rich in Custer County: Steal various items from the shelves at a Custer hardware store, attempt to get a cash refund for them, run from the store when the clerk becomes suspicious, get stopped and arrested in Newcastle, Wyoming with a carload of stolen property from two states, and oh yeah, have some marijuana on your person for good measure. Just ask the 34-year-old male and 41-year-old female from Newcastle, Wyoming how it worked for them. Did we mention other charges might be forthcoming after the Wyoming cops get done searching their house?

7:36 p.m.: Text message harassment revolving around the ownership of a hotly disputed cat was reported once again, at Trail View Apartments, in Custer. While attempting to sort out the situation over the telephone, a deputy was treated to a barrage of profanity by one person involved, who then hung up on him. It's nice to know the person is capable of handling this dispute like an adult.

11:42 p.m.: A suspicious man was reportedly sitting in a suspicious pickup at Custer elementary School. A deputy found the suspicious man to be a school janitor on his break.

4:07 a.m.: Theft of a van's back seat and other items was reported in the parking lot at Harney Street Apartments, in Custer. You'd have to be pretty low down to steal the back seat from a van.

9:02 a.m.: Teenagers were reportedly walking on thin ice (literally) at the lake near the city golf course. A deputy went there and made sure everyone made it to dry land.

5:18 p.m.: A resident on Clay Street, in Custer, reported running off a group of people who were amusing themselves by shooting each other with BB guns. It is hoped no one's eye was put out.

10:23 a.m.: A civil matter stemming from disputed grave decorations at a Custer cemetery was laid on the Sheriff's Office. It was definitely not a law enforcement problem.

9:03 p.m.: Someone called in, wanting a police escort from Custer to Rapid City, in case they had an anxiety attack while driving. Deputies were busy on actual criminal calls, so they were unable to assist.

***

7:01 p.m.: An angry male was reportedly cursing at fellow shoppers in the checkout line of a downtown Custer grocery store. The 41-year-old male from Skokie, Florida, was stopped by deputies a short distance away from the store and asked his side of the story. After a lot of bad noise, deputies sent the still-loudly complaining male on his way with a warning not to return to the store or face arrest.

7:51 p.m.: The vociferous visitor from Florida called Dispatch to complain about the way he had been treated. He apparently did not get the answers he wanted and ended the call by saying he was moving away the next day, because everyone he had dealt with were "a—holes." Don't go away mad, just go away.

***

8:13 a.m.: An anxious person dragged a deputy into a dispute at Trail View Apartments, over a book loaned to another person and then not returned. The title of the book was: "Don't Panic".

***

9:32 a.m.: Intentional damage to a vehicle was reported on Mount Rushmore Road, in Custer. Further investigation cast some doubt on the report's accuracy, but in the meantime…

9:48 a.m.: …the reporting person from the previous call, a 19-

year-old Custer male, was accused by a person on North Fifth Street of attempting to force his way into a residence there. The original reporting person was briefly detained by a deputy at the scene but was released after the residence owner declined to press charges, and then...

10:42 a.m.: ...the same 19-year-old Custer male appeared at an apartment at Trail View, demanding he be allowed to retrieve property kept there. After he did so, deputies ejected him from the premises. He should probably call it a day.

***

2:25 p.m.: An abandoned .32-caliber pistol was found in a booth cushion, at a downtown Custer restaurant. The sheepish owner of the feeble firearm showed up some time later to claim it.

9:14 p.m.: A deputy checked on a possibly unwanted person at a Custer motel. It turned out that the 49-year-old Hill City man was wanted, after all...for a couple of active arrest warrants.

7:38 a.m.: Attempted intentional damage was reported at a downtown Custer business. Someone appears to have a grudge against this particular building.

7:08 a.m.: Intentional damage in the form of aerosol-delivered cheese spread was reported on the sidewalk near the Custer Courthouse Annex. No one has yet caught the cheesy chumps.

11:43 a.m.: A stolen bicycle was reported on Washington Street, in Custer. The thief or thieves left another bicycle abandoned at the scene and rode away with one they apparently liked better.

2:24 p.m.: Bicycle-based harassment, "stupid signs", and "dogs with bad breath" were reported on Second Street, in Buffalo Gap, as part of a continuing neighbor versus neighbor conflict taking place there. Nothing that happened was against any kind of law.

6:27 p.m.: Trespassing was reported at a residence on Battle

Mountain Parkway: sinister surveying flags and suspicious stakes were apparently installed by an unknown person. The hunt is on for the suspects- possibly armed with a surveyor's transit and maybe maps.

***

5:33 p.m.: Numerous reports were received during the day of Klu Klux Klan leaflets strewn around the Custer area. The pathetic propagandists will face littering charges if caught.

8:32 a.m.: A "Grand Wizard" (whatever that is) of the aforementioned group called to say he would be talking to his followers about their previous methods of distributing propaganda in the Custer area. Hopefully, their methods won't involve continued lawn littering.

***

8:32 a.m.: Theft of a hunting blind was reported, on West Argyle Road. Apparently, it wasn't camouflaged well enough to keep the thieves from noticing it.

1:35 p.m.: Exhibition driving was reported on North Third Street, in Buffalo Gap. Charges are pending in this case. This incident also appeared to be part of the ongoing fracas in the area. Can't we all just get along?

2:08 p.m.: A person called the Sheriff's Office to find out if anyone had filed a petition to commit them for mental treatment. No one had, but if you have to ask...

11:07 a.m.: Here's a tip: If you dial 911 to find out if someone else in your house has called 911, you will probably get visited by cops who want to know what's going on. What was going on at a residence on Shooting Star Lane was apparently just a verbal argument between two people.

12:58 p.m.: Strange goings-on and international intrigue were reported at Trail View Apartments, in Custer. It is not clear what part of it is a law enforcement matter.

2:03 a.m.: Several people were observed throwing toilet paper and prophylactics on a vehicle parked in front of a downtown Custer tavern. After some investigation, the people were found to be preparing the car as part of an impending wedding.

12: THE MORAL OF THIS STORY SHOULD BE OBVIOUS

Some Sheriff's Log incidents go beyond average, everyday dumbness and become cautionary tales of "what not to do", hence the title of this chapter.

1:14 a.m.: A deputy on patrol in downtown Custer noticed two men walking down the street who tried to hide when they saw him. After hailing the two and identifying them, the deputy arrested one man for an active warrant. The moral of this story should be obvious.

10:53 a.m.: Deputies escorted a horse-drawn hearse and funeral procession through the downtown Custer area. While the procession was going on, a passing motorist decided he couldn't wait and attempted to pass it. A deputy pulled the 35-year-old Custer man over for a chat and discovered that he had an active warrant for his arrest. The moral here should be obvious.

8:54 p.m.: Reports were received of a fire at the STAR Academy West Campus. Deputies and fire units responded to the area, only to find the "fire" was actually part of an escape plan by one of the juvenile inmates. The juvenile apparently pulled a fire alarm and sprayed a fire extinguisher to divert the staff's attention while he ran. The juvenile was apprehended a short time later, near the campus. Apparently, the young inmate had not included putting on his shoes in the plan, so he was not able to get far in the woods.

12:09 a.m.: A deputy spotted two men on foot, carrying open beer bottles, on Mount Rushmore Road. When he doubled back to deal with them, the two attempted to hide from him, then dropped their bottles behind a bridge railing. The two were cited for open container and littering violations.

12:49 a.m.: Spray-paint damage was reported to a billboard on Highway 385, south of Custer. The incident is under investigation, but whoever spray-painted the graffiti could use a spelling lesson.

5:31 p.m.: Once upon a time in the Harney Street area, in Custer, two people were reportedly driving recklessly in their vehicles. The two reckless drivers stopped in the parking lot of a semi-popular convenience store to argue and shout at each other. Then, the two reckless drivers, a 47-year-old woman, and a 54-year-old man, were found by two deputies, who did some tests. The deputies found the two reckless drivers were also drunk drivers and took them to jail. The moral of this story should be obvious.
The End.

Thanksgiving Day, Thursday, November 27th

12:48 p.m.: Two upset women came to the door of a deputy's house in Fairburn, to report a possible case of domestic violence. The suspect had reportedly chased them into town with his vehicle. The suspect also arrived at the deputy's house a short time later, and the off-duty deputy promptly detained him at gunpoint. Other officers soon arrived, and after some investigation, arrested the suspect for simple assault, domestic violence.

7:43 a.m.: Intentional damage to signage from a carelessly-driven car was reported in a business parking lot in downtown Custer. A deputy found the culprit easily, as he had left his sign-damaged car in the same parking lot. The hapless hot-rodder was dealt with appropriately.

11:47 p.m.: Deputies checked on a suspicious vehicle parked on American Center Road. After giving the deputy a story about watching the stars, the driver, a 27-year-old Newcastle man, finally admitted he was waiting for a supposed girlfriend of his to leave a nearby residence. The man has been previously notified by the owners of the residence against trespassing. Deputies sent the star-crossed stargazer on his way.

4:13 p.m.: A possible assault was reported at a residence on Vilas Street, in Hermosa. After a deputy went there, the incident was found to likely have been just a mutual shoving match between two erstwhile friends. Both declined to press charges. However, the reporting person, a 50-year-old Hermosa woman, was found to be a wanted parole absconder, and was promptly arrested and held for the Department of Corrections.

8:36 p.m.: A deputy was stopped, dealing with a traffic violation on Highway 16, just south of Custer, when another vehicle sped by him too close. The deputy radioed ahead and had the car stopped for violating the "Move Over Law". After some investigation, one of the vehicle's occupants, a 20-year-old Hot Springs man, was arrested for possession of a controlled substance and possession of marijuana. The moral of this story should be obvious.

12:08 p.m.: Deputies arrested a 22-year-old Hermosa man for possession of a knife in the Custer County Courthouse. The man was apparently there to appear on another charge.

8:21 p.m.: A deputy serving civil papers at a residence on Deer Meadow Road noticed a person through the window of the residence that he knew to have a no-contact order barring him from being there. The man was spotted in the kitchen, apparently cooking supper. When the deputy knocked on the door, the man fled the room and attempted to hide in the back of the house. The deputy quickly detained 47-year-old Custer man and sent him to jail without his supper.

THE CUSTER COUNTY SHERIFF'S LOG

2:01 a.m.: A deputy stopped to get a tasty beverage at a semi-popular Custer convenience store noticed a car leave the parking lot in a reckless way. He followed the car, which left the area at a high rate of speed and eventually ended up in the driveway of a residence on Little Italy Road. The driver was initially non-compliant with the deputy, and other units responded to the scene. After some investigation, a Highway Patrol trooper arrested the driver for driving under the influence of alcohol and other charges. The moral of this story should be obvious.

12:57 a.m.: Deputies arrested a 21-year-old man for DUI after a traffic stop on Mount Rushmore Road, in Custer. Apparently, the man attracted the deputy's attention by over-driving the road conditions and losing control of his vehicle.

7:55 p.m.: A vehicle with a loud muffler was reportedly skulking around the Custer Highlands area, and shining a spotlight in a suspicious way. Deputies responded and cornered the sinister spotlight-shining skulker. The man turned out to only be looking for lost horses. He was also ticketed for not having a valid driver's license.

4:42 p.m.: Deputies working traffic on Highway 79 stopped a vehicle for a violation of the "Move over Law", near Hermosa. The deputies then arrested one occupant of the vehicle for an active warrant. The moral of this story should be obvious.

9:00 p.m.: Deputies responded to a disturbance call at a semi-popular Custer convenience store. By the time they arrived, those involved had left. A few minutes later, one of the suspects, an 18-year-old Custer boy, made the mistake of driving recklessly in front of the Custer YMCA, and an off-duty Highway Patrol trooper. The deputies wasted no time in issuing the man a ticket for exhibition driving and a warning to stay away from everyone else involved in the incident.

5:00 p.m.: Two people were reportedly fighting on the side of

Highway 40, east of Hermosa. A deputy investigated, finding only a verbal argument. However, one of the arguers had a warrant for his arrest and the other had a suspended driver's license. You can guess what happened to them.

8:54 a.m.: A deputy involved in another task observed a man known to have a suspended driver's license navigating a vehicle around downtown Custer. The man noticed the deputy and smiled and waved in a friendly way. That's nice. However, the man will likely not be smiling when his warrant for driving under suspension is served.

2:14 p.m.: A deputy stopped a 27-year-old Custer man and cited him for driving with a suspended license, on Highway 16A, just east of Custer. This is the man's third citation for this offense in two weeks. He does not appear to be learning his lesson.

6:01 p.m.: A deputy euthanized a wounded deer that was causing traffic problems near a Custer Golf Course. A large crowd of gawkers was also snarling the traffic flow. One person was apparently unhappy the deputy shot the deer and shouted profanities at him. The person was told to move along or face charges.

5:02 p.m.: Out of the mouths of babes: A small child called 911 and told the dispatcher to "shut the hell up" when she told him to put a parent on the line. A deputy went to the Custer residence that generated the call and had a long talk with the occupants about the proper use of the 911 system.

4:26 a.m.: Deputies went to a residence on Montgomery Street, in Custer, for a report of a man there "going crazy". Further investigation showed the man not to be crazy, but simply slobbering drunk. This is apparently the man's usual state, as deputies have found him passed out drunk in the gutter many times in the past. Deputies attempted to take the 33-year-old Custer man to the Detox. Facility in Rapid City but the man subsequently "talked himself into jail", or rather spit himself into jail, as well as threatening a deputy. To the man's surprise, both actions turned out to be against the law.

5:51 p.m.: Deputies investigated a possible domestic dispute... in front of the Sheriff's Office, in Custer. Further investigation showed only an verbal argument took place, but one of the participants, a 51-year-old Custer man was arrested for operating a motorcycle under the influence of alcohol.

1:16 a.m.: A deputy went to a Custer convenience store for a report of an argument between a clerk there and two customers. When the dust settled some time later, the deputy had arrested the original reporting person, a 28-year-old Custer woman, for a probation violation. The incident also became a minor theft investigation that turned into a major theft investigation. Numerous felony charges are pending on several former employees of the store. The reporting person may wish they had not made that phone call, after all.

***

10:23 a.m.: A gas drive-off was reported at a Custer convenience store at the corner of Fifth and Crook Streets. The vehicle was not found and would have likely never been searched for at taxpayer's expense, if the store asked for payment before turning on the pumps.

2:38 p.m.: Another Custer gas drive off was reported, on Mount Rushmore Road. The suspect was not found, either. *cough* pay before you pump *cough*.

4:48 p.m.: The gas drive-off mania continued in Custer, with another vehicle escaping from a convenience store on Fifth Street, that has failed to institute a pay before...ah, what's the use?

***

1:22 p.m.: A drunk driver was reported leaving a Custer

convenience store on North Fifth Street. A deputy followed the back to their home but found no reason to pull them over. However, the deputy did find the reporting person to have an active warrant, which he then dealt with.

4:42 p.m.: Deputies assisted an off-duty Highway Patrol trooper in administering a ticket to a deserving driver, just west of Custer, on Highway 16. You just never know who's in the car behind you.

10:26 a.m.: A deputy stopped a driver for a traffic violation on Highway 79, near Buffalo Gap. After receiving his citation, the driver chose to speed away. He chose poorly, as he received another citation once the deputy caught up to him again.

12:27 p.m.: Intentional damage to a security camera was reported at a downtown Custer tavern. Charges are pending on a spiteful suspect who was apparently upset at being refused service there. Not surprisingly, the incident was caught on camera.

7:17 p.m.: Someone called to report possible underage drivers at a semi-popular Custer convenience store. The responding deputy did not find the drivers but did discover the reporting person had a warrant for their arrest.

3:08 a.m.: Calling Attention to Yourself in a Bad Way, Part 1: Two traveling salespeople had a loud argument in front of their motel, on North Fifth Street, in Custer. When deputies arrived to investigate, they arrested one of the loudmouths, a 34-year-old Florida male, for an active warrant. The moral of this story should be obvious.

4:49 a.m.: Calling Attention to Yourself in a Bad Way, Part 2: A deputy on patrol in downtown Custer heard someone honking a loud air horn repeatedly. The deputy quickly tracked the honking to a vehicle being driven erratically around the downtown area and soon arrested the driver, a 33-year-old Belle

Fourche man, for DUI.

***

12:42 p.m.: Aggressive and suspicious salespeople were reported on Clay Street, in Custer. A deputy showed up and sent them on their way with a warning to do better business. However...

2:34 p.m.: ... a deputy dealt with the traveling hucksters again, on Pine Street, in Custer. The deputy ejected the group from the area, but when their boss showed up to collect the crew, the deputy arrested the 20-year-old South Carolina man for driving with a suspended license.

***

1:02 a.m.: Deputies attempted to keep the peace at a trailer park on Highway 16, west of Custer, while a former resident collected his belongings. The former resident was not able to keep his cool, and deputies eventually arrested the 36-year-old Custer man for disorderly conduct.

11:52 a.m.: A deputy noticed a vehicle pull onto the roadway, cutting off another car, near the STAR Academy West Campus, on Highway 385. After stopping the car, the deputy found it contained a female with no license and a male who was wearing pants with the word "INMATE" printed on them. After some investigation, the deputy found the 27-year-old Rapid City male was on an unofficial field trip, from an adult work detail at the nearby correctional facility. His trip continued...to jail.

12:16 a.m.: It was a case of good news and bad news for a 21-year-old Custer man walking along Mount Rushmore Road. The good news: A deputy stopped to offer the man a ride, as the temperature was below zero and the man was not dressed for the weather. The bad news: The man got a ride to jail, since he had active warrants for his arrest.

13: NAME THAT TUNE

I have a bad habit of jokingly referencing obscure song lyrics in the middle of otherwise normal conversations. This eventually spilled over into the Sheriff's Log- can you name that tune?

12:46 a.m.: Deputies were called back to Laughing Water Apartments, for a call of someone banging on a drum. The person was told to stop banging on the drum all day.

1:22 a.m.: A drunken man called 911 to report he was wasted and couldn't find his way home. The man was likely in the Custer area, but his directions were not very good, and he was not found.

5:38 a.m.: Wild, wild horses were reported on Highway 36, near Hermosa. The owner was contacted to drag them away.

10:38 p.m.: Deputies dealt with the same people at Valley-Hi Apartments, again. A possible disturbance was reported, but deputies found it to only be an intoxicated person loudly singing, "One Tin Soldier". Deputies told "Billy Jack" ride away for the night or face a ticket.

3:30 p.m.: Graffiti was reported behind a downtown Custer grocery store. An unknown person sprayed the word, "HALFBREED" on a wall with spray paint. It is not known if Cher has been interviewed as a suspect in this crime.

3:10 p.m.: "Hammer marks" were reported on a Woodlawn Drive residence, in Custer. It is not known when Hammer Time was, or whether the Hammerer in question was too legit to quit.

7:15 a.m.: A deputy checked the welfare of some people on Thunder Road. No moonshine, bootleggers, or any other problems were found there.

THE NIGHT SHIFT

After a few years of writing the original Sheriff's Log, Jason Ferguson, the general manager at the Custer County Chronicle, *asked me if I'd like to start writing a column every month or so for the editorial page. This became* The Night Shift. *The only guidance I got was "try to write something funny or smart". Sometimes I succeeded at this and sometimes I didn't.*

I'm still grateful they gave me the chance- especially since they had no idea what they were really in for.

ONE: WELCOME TO THE NIGHT SHIFT

When your day ends, my day begins.

As house lights go off, the stars sharpen into crystal points in the sky. The flow of traffic thins to a dribble, then stops. Only the creatures of the night, both animal and human, glide through the darkness between pools of electric light.

This is when I go to work.

Things are much sharper when you work at night. First impressions are quicker, conversations are blunter, and decisions are more instinctive. You know who your very few friends are. It is important to know who and where they are; it may take precious minutes and miles before they can help you. Sometimes it takes longer than that. On an unlucky and fateful night, it might take the rest of your life.

You don't think about that very much on the night shift, though. Other things occupy your mind: wanted people to keep an eye out for, paperwork to catch up on, homes and businesses to check on and...WHOA! Watch out for that deer crossing the road in front of you!

While you drive around the silent towns and the velvety dark woods, doing your job, listening to the radio, and thinking, you see and do things that normal people miss while they keep to their daylight routines. Your thoughts sometimes turn to the nature of the strange schedule you keep, and the things it does to you.

They say the night shift is unnatural. Turning nature's sleep and wake cycle on its head is a tough way to do things, say the experts on TV. Too much caffeine to stay awake through hours of boredom, punctuated by bursts of stress will take years off your life, the do-gooders chant. Like most things the do-gooders tell you, some of it's probably true, and some of it is…bull…err, not so true.

The night shift has its compensations though; those little secret things that make you feel smarter for having been up all night, instead of that crazy dumb feeling you get when the sun opens its baleful red eye over the prairie, your breath smells like old coffee, and your body signals that it's not very happy that you've tricked it again.

As compensation, I've seen the sharpest, most beautiful stars of my life. I've seen the moon shining so big and bright over fresh snow on the prairie that I could read by it. I've seen enough record-size deer and elk to make Boone and Crockett despair. I've seen coyotes, foxes, and mountain lions in droves. I've also seen some pretty amazing examples of the species we call humanity, perpetrating some of the most stupefying things you can imagine. Plus a few that you can't.

Some of these "stupid human tricks" are chronicled weekly in the *Sheriff's Log* of this very publication. Some of these things you see and hear while working the night shift can't be printed in a family newspaper. Some people exist just to serve as a bad example for everyone else.

There are good people that need you at night, too- people who call because they need someone to save their life, or to protect them, to take care of the problem that jolted them awake at this ungodly hour. There are good people that just need reassurance, or someone to talk to. That's another very good reason to keep staying up all night- because someone has to, and not everyone wants to.

It's all part of the package. You buy the ticket and you take the ride; hours of boredom punctuated by moments of sheer terror, set to a soundtrack of static-blurred AM talk radio. You're just another "Night Dog" cruising the city streets and rural gravel roads, looking for drunk drivers, burglars and mountain lions.

Have I been on the night shift too long? Am I too used to sleeping my days away and dealing with "interesting" people all night? Have I ingested too much liquid caffeine to ever think normally again? Why, that's ridiculous. I'm the same as I ever was.

Now if you'll excuse me, I've got work to do. Ever since I learned about the evil space aliens and their sinister plans on a late-night AM radio show, I've been perfecting a design for a tinfoil hat to keep the aliens from beaming thoughts into my head.

Pass the coffee.

TWO: DEALING WITH A FLASHLIGHT PROBLEM

Some people say I have a flashlight problem.

Maybe I do. Even as I sit here typing this, there are at least three flashlights on my person. I have one on my belt, one attached to my pistol, and one in my pocket of my 5.11 Tactical Pants, just in case (We'll talk about my "tactical pants problem" some other time). My car has at least three or four others in it. I'm not sure how many I own total. Probably more than twenty. Or thirty. But who's counting?

Now, having a flashlight handy does make sense- my job takes me to some dark places. Not dark in a metaphorical-darkness-of-the-human-soul way, but in a fall-down-the-basement-steps-of-somebody's-house-while-investigating-suspicious-noises way. And having a spare ready when the batteries die or the bulb burns out is a very good thing. But lately, when it comes to me and flashlights, the word "addiction" has been rearing its ugly head.

As a kid growing up, the only flashlights I had access to were made of tin or Tupperware and tended to give off a weak, yellowish light that was mostly good for seeing just enough of the basement stairs to fall down them anyway. Then, it happened. As an impressionable teenager, I was given an AA-battery-powered Mini-Maglite. It was so much better than the crappy throwaway ones I got as a kid. This was the first light I'd ever seen that didn't automatically disassemble itself into ten parts when you dropped it on the ground. It was machined from aluminum. It was tough. It was bright. It was... Tactically Cool.

Over the years, the addiction began to escalate. I got my hands on bigger lights with two, three, four, even six fat D-cell batteries in them. Once you held a six-cell D-battery light, you knew that was a real flashlight! It made a beam brighter than some car headlights. People flinched and muttered nasty things under their breath when you shined it at them. It was hefty piece of work. You could whack a vicious dog or a drunken malcontent with it if you needed to. This was great progress from the tin and Tupperware lights of childhood.

For a long time, the Maglite was the top of the flashlight heap around the Thompson Ranch. Then one day, something really bad happened. I discovered the Surefire light- a brand of "tactical" flashlight that caused my slide into full flashlight mania to speed up dramatically. These new lights were small, precise, and complicated. They were built with aerospace-quality hardware and used expensive lithium camera batteries. They were hellishly bright (and expensive).While carrying one of these lights, you might still fall down the basement steps, but you looked so...Tactically Cool... while you were falling down them.

At what point can you look back at yourself and say you've gone around the flashlight bend? Was it buying a flashlight that was worth a day's pay? Was it buying a flashlight that was so bright it could be seen through closed eye lids? How about the acquisition of a light that came with a warning that it could induce epilepsy in certain people? Not that I know anyone that's done those things, mind you.

In my case, it may have been the time I temporarily lost the flashlight that usually rode in my pants pocket. It ended up somewhere on the playground of my wife's old school in another state. When I was lamenting the loss of the light, she innocently asked if it would be worth paying a five dollar reward to the school kids to find it. She made a very strange face when I told her it would definitely be worth that, as the light had cost something like seventy-five dollars. I know now that look was not caused by indigestion.

Like they say, admitting you have a problem is the first step to overcoming it. Is there a local support group to help me come to grips with this flashlight problem? I'd better find out before it's too late, or my wife may be giving me that look again. I can picture the conversation now:

My Wife: "Honey, NASA called again today. They said to stop shining your eighteen-battery M1000X Super Tactical Dominator light at the International Space Station. It's making the crew dizzy. Isn't that light just a little…too bright?"

Me: "Hey, I can quit any time I want. Besides, it looks so…Tactically…Cool!"

THREE: WARNING- READING THIS COLUMN MAY CAUSE DROWSINESS

Recently, we decided that *The Night Shift* must list side effects and include a legal warning. Everything else does, in our sue-happy, it's-not-my-fault civilization, so this should come as no surprise. If you fall asleep or attempt to operate heavy machinery while reading this column, you are on your own, pal. Just remember, our lawyers play golf with your lawyers, so don't get cocky.

Is the western world getting out of hand with endless disclaimers and cautions? You be the judge-it wasn't enough that your prescription pill bottle carried dire dosage and side effects warnings. Now a mere TV commercial for any modern snake oil-in-a-tablet carries dire warnings that swallowing it could cause everything from an achy breaky heart to waking up dead. How about that well-known, uh, enhancement prescription with the two people in separate bathtubs? One interesting side effect warning that blares from the TV tube at any given hour about this elixir is that it sometimes may work *too well* and make a certain part of the male anatomy...well, work *too well* for four hours or more. Good to know if you take the stuff, but do we have to hear it on every commercial break?

The pickup truck I bought last year carried pages and pages of cautions, warnings, dire predictions and threats in a about a two-to-one mix with the parts that told me anything useful, like where the tire iron and jack were (Under the front seat, as I found on my own after lots of fumbling and cursing). My favorite was a baleful notation that I *should not drink alcohol and operate a motor vehicle*. I'm not sure who the target audience is for that warning; by the time you have enough money to buy a truck, you are probably aware that "road beers" are out of the question in said truck. If you're still drinking Coors in your cab, you probably already used the manual, along with its anti-DUI warning, to soak up your beer and bong water spills.

Speaking of drinking, let's talk about warnings on soft drinks. I've seen a plastic-bottled beverage that carries a screed against the dangers of *opening under pressure*. If this warning is to be believed, cracking the cap quickly could cause *serious injury*. Is there a legion of one-eyed, pirate-patch-wearing kids running around out there, caused by the horrors of opening soft drinks *under pressure*? Please, point them out. But don't point too quickly. You might put someone's eye out, like I heard happened somewhere, swear to God it did, man. I read about it on the Internet, so it *must* be true.

My absolute favorite legal warning and disclaimer comes from Apple, the people who are terrifically proud they make something like 1% of the computers used in America, and a little gadget called an IPod that plays music. While downloading some music for an IPod, I was heartened and encouraged to see that the Apple and their fearless corporate attorneys are doing their part to keep America safe in the Global War on Terror (or whatever the White House prefers to call it this week).

Before I could set up an account or listen to any music, I had to agree to the following keep-the world-safe statement: *"Licensee also agrees that licensee will not will not use the Apple Software for any purposes prohibited by United States Law, including without limitation, the development, design, manufacture or production of nuclear missiles, or chemical or biological weapons."*

If you don't think this is important, just imagine the scene inside a musty Al-Qaeda cave somewhere on the frontier between Afghanistan and Pakistan, with the following exchange taking place between two smelly, bearded men:

Smelly, Bearded Man #1: "Habib, it's come to my attention you have been using your IPod to help plan *Operation Grand Slam,* our plan for final nuclear and chemical victory against the infidels. I want you to stop. Your license agreement with I-Tunes *forbids* it!"

Smelly, Bearded Man #2: "Achmed, you are right! I would prefer cluster bombs to be dropped on my head, or to be locked away at Guantanamo Bay forever, rather than face the might of *Apple lawyers.* They make even a *true martyr* afraid!"

Maybe the solution to all this spiraling safety-first simpering would be to equip each person with a warning and disclaimer when they're born, just to be safe: *"Warning! Life is not certain. There is no guarantee that you will be happy or amount to anything. No matter what happens, you will likely have to suck it up and deal with it. Side effects may include drowsiness, death and taxes. Void in some states."*

FOUR: THE STREET COP'S SUPERSTITION SWEEPSTAKES

"Step on a crack, break your mother's back!" goes the old saying. Even in our modern digitally-drenched, computer-controlled, scientific society, most average people are a little superstitious.

Whether it's saying "Bless you!" when someone sneezes, throwing a pinch of salt over your shoulder after spilling some, or feeling uneasy about whistling past a graveyard, lots of otherwise rational people develop little tricks and habits to ward off bad luck and random evils.

Like most cops, I'm more than a little superstitious. The Job makes you this way.

I now know that it's considered a mortal curse to tell the oncoming shift of night dogs anything to the effect of "It's really quiet out there," or, "Ah, nothing's gonna happen tonight." You're sure to be met with a chorus of groans and rough speculation about your state of mental health. Not to mention a few choice comments about your family tree.

Most experienced cops are absolutely sure in their darkest heart of hearts that all really important calls that involve staying on duty a bunch of extra hours take place within a few minutes of the end of their shift. The probability of getting the "money call" increases if you need to use the bathroom, if you are hungry, if your patrol car is low on gas, or if you forgot some crucial piece of equipment on the kitchen table or in the lockbox at the jail. (Hey, has anybody seen my gun? Come on now, this isn't funny anymore!)

If you really want to double down on the superstition

sweepstakes, extra points are added for the last shift before a weekend, the last shift before a vacation, and very possibly, the last shift before retirement, as fabled in numerous Hollywood cop-buddy movies: "Wow, tough break for Murtaugh. He had thirty years in already. Too bad he got stuck with the suicidal burnout from Narco, huh?"

Years ago, at another department, I was considered to be the bringer of bad luck. Being young and cocky, I would talk about how nothing was happening and how I wanted some good-old fashioned, red-blooded American action! Like any young rookie I longed for car chases, bar fights, family feuds, and all the other fun-loving festivities found on weekend nights in Anytown, USA. I would often taunt the older (and little did I know at the time) wiser cops by telling them that there was fifteen minutes left in our shift, and not to worry, something good could still happen. Often, I'd hardly closed my trap before a call crackled over the radio, and we were off to deal with something that would keep us busy for the next several hours.

Whether it was true or just a result of my relentlessly running my mouth, the other cops began to believe that it could be quiet for days, but when I showed up to work, the wheels would fall off their calm situation in short order. I would say that I don't mean that the wheels literally fell off anything, except a wheel actually did fall off a patrol car I was in once. Did I already mention the other cops thought I was the bringer of bad luck?

Slowly, the relentless grind of street life began to force me to change my attitude about taunting the fickle finger of fate. Certain incidents that happened to me could have been what we in law enforcement call "clues".

One of these eye-openers happened on a frosty fall night. I had just installed myself into the passenger seat of a patrol car and got comfortable as we pulled out of the parking lot. The other officer told me that it had been a very slow shift so far. I said that was about to change now that I was there. Suddenly, every street and house light we could see blinked out, plunging us into darkness. My fellow law dog said: "Now you did it."

Technically, that wasn't true. A drunk driver who smashed into several mailboxes, a motel sign, and finally a power pole was responsible for the power outage that shut off the power to half the town. I knew what the other cop meant, though. In the night-shift world, everything is connected. There are no coincidences.

Today, ten years or so later, I try not to tempt fate any more than I have to. My gas tank is full, my bodily functions are promptly taken care of, and I try to make sure I have all the equipment I need to get through a shift.

I'm careful of what I say, too. When someone tells me it's been a quiet night or a really slow shift, my answer is always the same: "So far."

OFFICER LUMPY JOINS THE NIGHT SHIFT

After churning out The Night Shift *in the usual mundane columnist way for a while, I began hear from some of my fellow cops about what they thought of the things I was writing about. The stuff they had to say was actually funnier and more true to the night-shift world than the dreck I had been dredging out of my caffeine-pickled, sleep-deprived brain.*

They needed a voice- which eventually surfaced as "Officer Lumpy", a composite of a whole bunch of crusty, hard-drinking, "been-there-done that" old-time street cops I'd worked with during a quarter-century of various kinds of adult-babysitting-type jobs. In time, he started to speak for himself, as a counterpoint to my younger, still-naive "College Boy" persona in many of the columns.

Many years of police life later, my wife pointed out that I now more closely resemble Officer Lumpy than the College Boy, both in appearance and attitude. She's not wrong.

ONE: A PREEMPTIVE APOLOGY FOR 2010

I was drinking beer with an old cop buddy of mine on New Year's Eve. My buddy has more years on a few different adult-babysitting-type jobs than he'd care to count anymore, not to mention a few suspensions without pay and a few ex-wives. He doesn't work around here, and to further protect the guilty we'll refer to him as "Officer Lumpy".

After a few bottles of Coors the other night, Lumpy told me he wants everyone to know he's sorry. "Sorry for what?" I asked.

"I'm sorry for everything that's gonna happen this year," said Lumpy. "Ya know, every time I'm gonna say something some jackass doesn't like. When I arrest somebody an' they don't like it. When I don't arrest somebody an' somebody else don't like it. When I write some guy a ticket an' he gripes to the boss. When I don't write somebody a ticket an' the other guy gripes to the boss. All that stuff."

I thought about this for a beer or two. In his own way, Lumpy was right. We live in an "apology culture" these days. Someone more poetic than me said that we live in an age where nothing is a surprise, but everything is an outrage. I said this to Lumpy and not surprisingly, he agreed with me.

"Look," He said, stifling a beery belch. "It's kinda sick. All kinds a people are wandering around the world just waiting to be offended at whatever. Things they see on TV. Things they read in the paper. Things other guys say to them. It's like they got an Offense-o-Meter built into 'em. It goes ding, ding, ding and they shoot into full outrage mode. Pretty soon they're spouting all kinds of stuff: wantin' a public apology. Wantin' a written apology. Cryin' to the boss. Whatta bunch of crap." He punctuated this with another drink of beer and finally let the belch go. When the rumbling had subsided, he continued.

"Like I was saying, I didn't go to college. I ain't a law professor, but last time I checked, I'm pretty sure there ain't an amendment to the Constitution that says
we got a right not to be freakin' offended. You ever saw that one, college boy?"

I admitted I had not seen that amendment to the Constitution, either. Of course, I've been accused of taking that inspired document a little too literally, especially the Amendment that comes right after the First (I like all the Amendments, but that one's my favorite). Lumpy was right about lots of people assuming they have a God-given right not to be angered or offended by what they see and hear. A quick check of the news on any day will find somebody being loudly outraged about what another person said or did: a second-rate talk-show host making an off-the-cuff statement about a basketball team's hair, someone possibly flushing a Koran down the toilet at a prison in Iraq, bumper stickers on cars that offend people, T-shirts they don't like, and so on. The list is literally endless and ongoing.

Usually, the "offender" is shouted down or shamed to the point that they slink into the spotlight with a quick, vaguely-worded mea culpa, and the members of the apology culture pack up their portable outrage and troll for new targets. Meanwhile, the value of actual humility and actual forgiveness drops to nothing, as the pervasive "gotcha" attitude drips down to normal people in the normal world. The average person can't get through their day without apologizing about most of the things they do and feigning some kind of guilt.

Lumpy reminded me of his favorite public incident of manufactured outrage from a few years back: "You remember when we were running low on ammo to send to the guys in Iraq, so we bought some from the Israelis? Somebody started sniveling about how that was gonna offend everyone in Iraq if we were shooting ammo made by Jewish people, so the Army took everyone's bullets back. Holy crap! We can shoot bullets at people and kill 'em, but don't offend 'em! That might hurt their little feelings"

After a few more beers and a few more belches, Lumpy put a fine point on the whole discussion.

"I can tell this years gonna be just as bad as 2009", Lumpy said. "Tell the people that read your phony-baloney column in that newspaper that they can just relax if I make 'em mad this year. I know they're just waiting for an excuse to whine and snivel about what I'm doing. So tell 'em that if they see me driving too fast to a call or I don't show up to their call in time or if they don't like how I'm talking 'em, they can relax. Tell them I'm already sorry. Does that make 'em happy already?"

Does it?

TWO: YOU SAY YOU WANT A REVOLUTION?

"I got your revolution right here, pal!"

Lumpy was grinning crookedly at me around an unlit cigar from his seat in a booth in the back of the local stop-and-rob store. He and the clerks had formed an uneasy truce: the old street monster wouldn't fire up his evil stogies inside as long as the crew kept his personal coffee pot full.

I slid into the booth across from Lumpy and followed his gaze to the flat-screen TV on the wall. The streets of Cairo, Egypt were echoing with the roar of peaceful change, via a cable news network. Or maybe the streets were echoing with the roar of a radical Islamist mob takeover. No, wait! I've got it: The streets were echoing with the sinister roar of a disguised military coup.

If you were just as confused over the true nature of the chaotic events in the land of pyramids and sand, you're not alone. Pretty much every public agency in Washington issued their own version of the facts, without calling anyone else to get their stories straight first. Ever heard that thing about a thousand monkeys punching away at a thousand typewriters eventually writing a Shakespeare play through blind luck? Nobody in D.C. came up with a "Midsummer Night's Dream", but some of it was high comedy nonetheless.

I was still unsure what we were really watching unfold in the glittery plasma picture and told Lumpy as much. He snorted. "I jist heard some little TV reporter babe gushin' all over about this whatever-tha-hell-it-is-in-the-streets," Lumpy said. "She calls it "people power". It musta slipped right through her green-tinted sixties mind that them "people" were wearin' camouflage uniforms and drivin' tanks."

"Lumpy, you've got a good point." I said. "The army was the real power in Egypt before all these demonstrations started. They have been ever since Nasser and some other military officers took over the place more than fifty years ago. It doesn't really matter who the figurehead is at the top, because the generals call the shots."

"Yer right, college boy," said Lumpy. "All this 'democracy' stuff them demonstrators are talkin' is just crap. I mean, ol Hosni's out tha door like they wanted but they got a general tellin' 'em what to do now. What's the difference? An' I saw on TV tha other day that this general told them Egyptians they couldn't go on strike and to go home. Some democracy.

"Everybody on TV wanted this ta be some kinda hippie revolution or somethin'. All them Geritol-eatin' sixties rejects on TV were runnin' around all starry-eyed and slack-jawed, talking the same crap they were talkin' then. It's just wishful thinkin', ya know. The world don't really work that way but lots of them guys took too many pills and they still fall for this stuff. Hell, I blame the Beatles. You say ya want a revolution? Somebody shoulda torpedoed their yellow submarine."

I thought about that for a minute while we drank our coffee. "I wouldn't go that far, Lumpy. It isn't all for nothing. Once people get a taste of freedom, they don't want to go back. Look at what happened in all the old communist countries in the 90's; once they started earning money in a free market and buying and selling what they wanted for themselves, it was all over. McDonald's won over Marx every time."

Lumpy smiled. "Maybe you got somethin' there. It all comes down to tha money, don't it? Those guys in Egypt might get somethin' outta this after all. I'll tell ya what, though, it has been fun to watch on TV.

"You know the best part of the whole deal was that counter attack by Hosni's gang of camel-ridin' thugs. Hell, I nearly wet myself watching five a them scruffy broomstick-totin' bozos tryin' to waylay one a them dudes swinging a pipe from camelback. Nobody won that time. Didn't look like anyone even got hurt much. but boy it sure made that camel mad. You ever hafta catch a mad camel? Lemme tell ya, llamas got nothin' on em!"

"How do you know that, Lumpy?" I said, curious about Lumpy's camel expertise.

Lumpy began his story: "There was this drunk carny that crashed tha circus truck on Highway 11, outside a Ord, Nebraska, back in…well, it was a while ago, in the dead a winter. And when we got there, there were all these circus animals running around…"

I should have known.

THREE: LUMPY SAYS GOODBYE TO THE CROWN VIC

My old cop friend, Officer Lumpy, was drinking coffee and sulking at his usual corner table in the back of the local stop-and-rob the other day. I slid onto a chair across from him and poured myself a cup. At first, I didn't notice anything wrong; sulking is one of Lumpy's two or three usual moods.

Then I noticed the crumpled up tissues on the table in front of him, jumbled in with the spilled coffee puddles and cruller crumbs. I looked at his weather-beaten, puffy face. His eyes were red. Had Lumpy been crying? It usually took a bottle or two of the sauce to get him all weepy, but here he was, all red-eyed at three in the afternoon, apparently sober.

"So, who divorced you this time, Lumpy?" I asked.

He looked at me with his beady, red-rimmed eyes and said, "Ford Motor Company, that's who." He shoved a wrinkled copy of Police and Fleet Manager Magazine toward me. "Those bozos are going to quit makin' the Crown Vic!"

For those of you who aren't tuned in to the everyday cop world, Lumpy was lamenting the planned halt of Ford Crown Victoria production. Since the '70's the big Blue Oval battle cruiser had been a fixture in most of the police departments across the nation. For a few years, in the dark days of the late nineties, the Crown Vic was the only police car you could buy.

"Oh, yeah," I said. "I read something about that. Ford's closing the production line for the Crown Victoria cars in 2011 because no one drives them but old people and cops. But they're coming out with another 'Police Interceptor' car to replace it."

Lumpy howled with rage. "Replace it? Police Interceptor? Read this freakin' article!" He scrabbled back a few pages and showed me a slick car company promotional picture of a black-and-white patrol car with a couple of unbelievably good looking actors dressed in phony cop uniforms posed around it. I snorted at the posers in the picture. Neither one looked like he'd been in a fist fight since junior high. Lumpy continued. "It says 'Police Interceptor' on the side, but it's a stinking Taurus underneath. A Taurus! It's a clown car, not a police car!"

I like to get Lumpy going sometimes; it's very entertaining and it alarms innocent bystanders. I started to play devil's advocate. "Oh, come on, man. The Taurus is a perfectly good car. It's got a high-output V-6 engine and front wheel drive so it gets good traction in the slick stuff. I'm sure it gets really good gas mileage, too."

Lumpy stared at me like I'd just suggested he strip off his uniform and jump into the Cheyenne River. "Holy crap, you almost said that with a straight face. You been spending too much time in the office toadyin' to the brass. See, but I remember what you were drivin' when you first started at that department, rookie."

I cringed. As I new cop I'd been sentenced to a year or so in Chevy's so-called "police package" clown-car, the Impala. Lumpy sensed my discomfort and closed in for the kill. "I remember you sayin' something about hitting your head on the door every time you got in or out. And it sat so low you scraped every driveway and curb in town while you were on patrol. And the time you were running hard to that hot call and the engine started smoking..."

"That's enough." I held up my hand. Lumpy had got me.

"Yeah, I felt pretty low when I saw this article. But I cheered up for a little while," said Lumpy. "Ford lost their mind, but Dodge has the Charger. It ain't as big as the Vic but it goes like a freakin' rocket sled. And Chevy's bringin' back the full-size Caprice next year. With a big six-liter, aluminum block V-8 engine. Now that's a cop car.

"So, I went in to the boss and ast him what we were gonna buy to replace our Vics when they wear out." Lumpy said. "The good news was he didn't wanna buy that new Taurus crap-box. Then I saw the bad news." Lumpy pulled out a crumpled promotional sheet that advertised the new police-package Ford Explorer and spread it on the table.

"The boss says, come on Lumpy, it's holds more gear than a car but you can drive it faster than a truck. He calls it a 'crossover'. I say, that's funny, I thought a crossover was one a those guys that dresses up in women's clothing and trolls around bars. That's when he threw me outta his office."

FOUR: ONE OUT OF FIVE

I was sipping carbolic café coffee the other day in a little town in another county the other day, when my old cop buddy came swaggering in with a creak of worn gun leather and the faint odor of old cigar smoke. You might know him; his red boozer's nose and foghorn voice usually warn everyone in the room he's inbound and their peaceful day is about to take a turn for the worse. That's right, it was Officer Lumpy- and contrary to popular belief, only his middle name is Trouble.

The waitress picked up her step and quickly got Lumpy's coffee cup filled and positioned in front of him. She knew what problems were likely to descend on the place if the constant stream of caffeine to the old street monster's head was interrupted.

Through the cloud of steam connecting his mouth to the cup, Lumpy said, "Hey, I been lookin' for ya. I read that thing you wrote in the newspaper last month about the taxes an' how it sucked you were going to pay more next year. It was pretty good. But then, I heard some people cryin' about how you didn't know what you were talkin' about and whatnot. I heard you were kinda down about it."

I admitted the column was written quickly in a flash of anger and could have been edited a bit to make my points about limited government more effectively. "Lumpy, what ticked me off was that all some folks could do was carp and say that I should be happy to pay lots of taxes to make bigger and bigger government and that I should shut up because I work for the county. I thought they were missing the point that too much of our local money was going to Washington to disappear forever. It doesn't matter who you work for, it's not right."

Lumpy was nodding. "Yeah, yeah, I know all that already. Yer always sayin' that stuff and for my money, you're right. But, listen, I figured out what's up with all whiny I-love-big-nanny-do-everything-for-me-government types." Lumpy pulled a crumpled newspaper article from his threadbare jacket pocket. A few rounds of loose .357 Magnum ammunition fell out with it, bouncing on the table. "Leave it there," said Lumpy. "I got no change for the tip."

The article was headlined: ONE IN FIVE AMERICANS MENTALLY ILL. It went on to posit the idea that twenty percent of the population sought some kind of mental treatment last year. Or should have gotten it, or thought they needed it. To me, it looked like the article was lashed together around a couple of press releases from some snarky group of do-gooders and shimmed up with shaky statistics and slim documentation. It was the kind of article that would run opposite an ad for an antidepressant drug; typical big-city newspaper stuff.
Lumpy was a believer, though.

"Look, it explains where them tax-me-please guys come from. They ain't right in the head." He smacked the table for emphasis, spilling coffee and rattling cartridges. "Who wants to pay more taxes an' see 'em go to deadbeats? It'd be like me volunteerin' to pay my ex-wives more alimony!"

"Now, Lumpy, that's going too far. Those people aren't crazy. They just see things differently than we do and they're just speaking their minds. Besides, twenty percent of Americans can't be mentally ill. That figure is just hype." I said.

Lumpy's laugh started from deep in his large belly and rumbled upward until it came out his weather-beaten mouth. "Hype? These crazy people are all over the place. They're always doin' stuff you can't explain. Hell, I jist saw one a them 'one-in-five' guys on the Interstate coming in here. He sat in the passing lane, in his little Prius, just hangin' in my blind spot, for miles, talkin' on his little smarty phone. He musta been crazy. He really jumped when I mashed on the brakes an' he shot right by.

"Or how 'bout them mouth breathers in Wally Mart that go the wrong way down the aisles, cut ya off, have their little trailer park reunion right in the middle and all yer tryin' to do is get your beer and pizza back to your car? They gotta be crazy. One in five. I'm tellin' ya, they're out there." Lumpy was getting really worked up, now.

The waitress rolled her eyes when she came around to refill our empty coffee cups. "Bullets for a tip, again?"

I looked around the restaurant and laughed. I counted the waitress, two other customers and me. Lumpy made number five. It shouldn't surprise anyone.

FIVE: LUMPY GIVES FIRE DIRECTIONS

I was directing traffic on the highway the other day, where a forest fire was threatening the roadway and several surrounding housing developments. A few fellow law dogs and myself had been stranded on the pavement there for the last few hours, coughing in the smoke, answering good questions and dumb questions, giving directions, yelling into the radio, looking for lost homeowners, coordinating the rescue of dogs, cats and grandmothers and sweating a lot.

Like moths to the flame or liberals to other people's money, lots of folks are drawn to a fire. Homeowners, neighbors, relatives, friends, acquaintances, media personalities, slack-jawed gawkers, brittle do-gooders and nose-picking, unaware tourists are all people you can expect to wash up against your traffic control point. Every single one of these classes of folks has a really, really, *really* good reason they need to get through your roadblock, *right now*!

You can sympathize with the homeowners and relatives; they're in a terribly uncertain situation with loved ones or a house on the fire line. You do whatever it takes to help them. As for the rest of the people that show up, they mostly don't get what they want, which is to get past the roadblock, gawk at the fire, overdose on pine smoke, get in the firefighters' way and generally be a pain in the rear.

As the sun began to set in the smoky, fire-streaked sky, I was arguing with one of the hard cases at the roadblock, a slightly-stylish and arrogantly-assured woman in a Toyota Prius with

California plates and a "Coexist" bumper sticker. She didn't want to take a different route to see Mount Rushmore and why wouldn't I just let her go through? She had to get there before the lighting ceremony, you see. I was telling her my final answer for the third time, when I heard a familiar boozy baritone behind me: "Hey lady! They don't have forest fires in Commie-fornia? D'you argue with the CHP like this? Just turn it around and go hug some trees, why dontcha?"

I turned, and yes, it was my old buddy, Officer Lumpy. He had a can of Coors in one hand and a slice of what looked like sausage-and-cheese pizza in the other. He was out of uniform, wearing old jeans, a Hawaiian shirt, beat-up cowboy boots and a crap-eating grin. The woman looked at him as if he'd just dropped out of a UFO. She'd never seen anything like him. It was obvious she didn't want to see any more, as she executed a quick U-turn and sped off, the sad little Prius engine wheezing its anger at having to actually burn gasoline, instead of hope and change.

"Where the hell did you come from?" I asked Lumpy as he tore another chunk out of his pizza pie and swallowed some more Rocky Mountain spring water and barley. I didn't see his old rust-and-blue-colored Jeep pickup anywhere. He grinned wolfishly.

"Well...I was goin' to Deadwood to play some cards, drink some beer, but I heard ya out here hollerin' at idiots an' thought ya might need some help. So I jumped in the Red Cross van an' they dropped me here. Ya want some pizza, college boy? I think the Red Cross guys brought a whole air-drop pallet fulla it."

I was very happy Lumpy had appeared and not just because he brought pizza. After all, he didn't even work for my department. He was just another "lookie-loo" at a place full of glassy-eyed spectators. Whatever he said or did was not my problem and liable to be very entertaining. As we scarfed down our pizza, another carload of tourists rolled up. They were from one of those states that grow a lot of corn; I forget which. After telling them they had to turn around, due to a forest fire, the driver asked, "Well, what started it?"

Lumpy said, "What are we, the fire marshals? Do I look like that albino jackrabbit S.O.B. on the freakin' C.S.I Miami show? Hey, wait, Forensics called an' said it was started by a combination a oxygen, heat an' fuel." The corn-state traveler got a pinched look on his face like he was suddenly constipated and motored off.

Next, we got a twitchy woman who just *had* to return to her second-cousin's house to get "important papers" she had forgotten when she evacuated. I repeated our orders that no one was allowed back in due to the fire conditions. She began telling me that she knew a fellow cop, so we should let her in. Lumpy piped up: "Yeah? I know that guy too. That dirty so-and-so was two-timing me with my second ex-wife. I hate his guts." Suddenly the twitchy woman decided she didn't really need to go in, after all and slunk away. I looked questioningly at Lumpy; he laughed. "Actually, that ain't true. She was two-timin' some other flatfoot. But it sends 'em down the road, don't it?"

Lumpy and I were still laughing when a minor local media figure pulled up in his live-news-as-it-happens-mobile. He broadsided us with his real-TV-announcer's-voice: "It's imperative we be allowed in to film the fire, right away!" Lumpy's grin began to form. It sped up and swept from one side of his face to the other, like the fire on the hill above us.

"Hey, bud. I remember *you*. Yer the guy that useta get drunk an' skinny-dip in tha town fountain with yer weather guy, ol' whats-his-name..."

As the Famous Anchorman's face began lose all its color, I thought to myself that it was going to be a great night, after all.

RALLY OF THE DAMNED

In August of 2014, I was between "real" police jobs.

As part of my strange work year, I submitted no less than six different tax documents from various private and public employers. During that "gypsy cop" phase of my career, I spent nine days as a temporary deputy at the 74th Sturgis Bike Rally.

Growing up in the Black Hills, I'd seen Sturgis Rallies before, but never like this: wearing a uniform, a badge, a gun, and riding in the right-hand seat of a black Ford Police Interceptor SUV. From the belly of the beast, as it were. It was a hell of a view; so much so, that I figured I'd better take notes.

Please note: Unlike the previous section of this book, this piece wasn't written for a family-friendly newspaper, so it contains rough language and a lot of dirty street stuff. That gritty mix was part of the whole week, and to omit it or sugar-coat it would dull the experience- as well as leave behind some of the truth.

1. FRIDAY

The crowd straggles in.

Subtle rumble, like the sea, in the background. Slowly building. Thousands of engines. By the hour it gets louder...louder... louder. It won't stop for another week.

No One to Run With by the Allman Brothers Band was running through my head. Too bad I missed those guys in concert when they were here a few years back.

Writing speeding tickets on Highway 79 in the shadow of Bear Butte. One, two, three. Third one almost drunk. No jail- we gave the *one drink away from disaster* speech to an aging insurance salesman/badass biker from Sioux Falls and his girlfriend. A ride to their campground with us, a tow truck for their machine. We hustled back to the office, but missed most of the nightly briefing. Too bad.

Rally Rumors: The Sioux Warrior Society is planning to picket Ted Nugent's concert at a big mega-saloon. No clue of their beef with the Motor City Madman. It might be an interesting night.

More Rumors: Camera drones are a big problem on Main Street this year- at least in the feverish minds at the FAA. They have been bearding every chief cop in the area about the *Danger of Drones*, especially *Drones Without Their Papers*, and to tell any drone operators to stop or be arrested. A good-natured discussion ensues among the cops about the proper way to shoot down drones. Shotguns loaded with buck? Pistols? Big fly swatters?

Supper is buffet-style sandwiches from a mass of bread, cold cuts, and all the trimmings, in the break room. Later, peanut butter and jelly at 9 pm, along with fresh chocolate-chip cookies, chips and cold lemonade. This is *good* cop food- it beats the usual convenience store roller-grill tripe.

Back on the road. Seen on the front seat of a car, during a traffic stop: a roll of toilet paper and half a banana cream pie still in the pan...let the good times roll.

The Rally smells like: exhaust, burning rubber, hickory smoke, campfire smoke, sweat, cigarettes, beer...

Bang! 90 miles per hour in a 55 zone. And drunk, drunk, drunk! A blood-alcohol content of .242! That's like three times the legal limit. That's drunk! Can you even balance a bike at that BAC? The guy, handcuffed in the back seat, mumbling, asks us if we can drop him off at his campground, instead of jail. No. Would we take a hundred bucks to drop him off at the campground? Umm...no. Back to town and to jail we go. Our first drunk driving arrest of the Rally. And it's a felony third-offense. Good stuff to start off our week.

Fight at the Fort Meade reservoir, everyone scattered...a golf cart crash with injuries (more drunks again) at the Glencoe campground...packs of howling drunks, stoners and assorted scrotes wander the streets of Sturgis, below the police building, after bar closing time. The rumble of bikes gets stronger, even in the hazy early morning hours, as the sun staggers up over the Black Hills.

Things are picking up. The 74th Sturgis Bike Rally has begun.

2. SATURDAY

"Motorcycles are everywhere," says the bumper sticker... Yeah, they're *everywhere*; driving like *idiots.*

"But the map says these roads are paved! Look, the gray line shows a paved road! We didn't know there were gravel roads out here when we left California."
–Lost and clueless riders on a county road.

"Okay, I was *staring at your tits but it's because there's a* gigantic pot leaf *tattooed on one of them."*
–a cop to a passenger at a traffic stop.

***

Cutting people off in traffic is uncool... Cutting off two cops in a marked police car is just ignorant. And ticket-worthy. Ask that middle-aged lady from Minnesota playing biker dress-up if she needs bigger mirrors on her Harley.

How drunk do you have to be to fall asleep in a tent pitched on a lawn in downtown Sturgis, what with shouting yahoos, roaring bikes and general chaos at all hours? A blood alcohol content of .200 or better helps. You feel pretty low in the morning, though.

Back on Highway 79 North, two lanes of blacktop between the out-of-town Rally campgrounds. The cops call it "running the gauntlet", because the Highway Patrol troopers spend most of their time there. In ten miles, you could see four or five traffic stops...every time, all night.

We decided things were too crowded and moved off to the Interstate 90 Service road, two lanes, down the hill from a campground on the outskirts of Sturgis. Three traffic stops in a row: bang-bang-bang, and then...

We clear from the last stop, pull back onto the road and...HOLY SHIT, THAT PICKUP IS IN OUR LANE! A high-speed slalom course between a converted school bus (Da Bus), two bikes, and a pickup driving on the wrong side of the road, coming right at us. The bus passengers cheered when we flipped on our lights and siren- the guy had apparently been tailgating them for miles and finally got up the courage to pass them in a no-passing zone...in front of a police car. The pickup driver? Stupid, but sober. Lucky for him.

Lights and siren, back down the valley for a domestic fight at the No Name Campground. A white-knuckle run, clogged intersections and clueless drunk bike riders everywhere, even after midnight. We arrived...He said, she said, they said. They're all lying. Put it in the mix: King Budweiser, hand-rolled cigarettes, and a wanna-be, semi-pro stripper with baby mama drama. The other half of the dispute, the guy was drunk with a southern accent, a no-extradition warrant for assault and battery from another state, and a lousy Kel-Tec 9mm pistol. After a lot of bad noise – no one was really breaking the law- the whole mess was resolved by separation. We carted the female off to the women's shelter for the night.

More late calls, more paperwork, made us late getting off duty. Little did we know, we never would leave on time, for the next seven days.

3. SUNDAY

"I don't believe it...there goes that shitbox Dodge again!"

–a cop. (A cool replica of the Bluesmobile, driven by two dudes dressed up like Jake and Elwood was spotted at a bar in Piedmont... But we weren't authorized to use Unnecessary Violence, so they got away.)

***

So you're going 72 miles per hour in a 45 zone, testing your Harley's new turbocharger kit? It must be working...say, you got 220 bucks on you, bro? Otherwise, we'll have to do the paperwork at the jail. Your bike will be waiting for you at the tow yard.

Local drama in Blackhawk. Stupid drunk guy was staying in the garage next door to his "boss", selling meat door to door. They also live next to a bar...handy for him: drunk guy got even drunker there, crashed into the house through a back window and passed out on the couch. To jail he went. Every door-to-door meat man I've ever dealt with is a shady fucker. Every one of them.

Downtown Sturgis on a quiet Sunday night: A churning mob of humanity, motors, smoke, and loud music. A gigantic open-air insane asylum for people with money.

The 8- ball of coke fell out of the guy's pants pocket in the jail booking room: "Hey. I don't know how that got there. I just borrowed those this morning. These aren't my pants." No problem, the jail staff has some snazzy new orange ones for you.

Standing outside the law-enforcement building at 2 a.m.: All the city cops' foot patrols straggle in from Main Street, sweaty, disgusted, tired... The motorcycle cops and the tow trucks take over the streets along with the garbage trucks and the street sweepers.Lots of yelling, the rumbling of bike engines, and a lot of cursing as one of the outlaws is shuffled off the street by his more sober buddies. The cops took his bike, instead of taking him and the bike. Rally rules: every fucking bike is off the fucking street at ten minutes past two fucking AM, or it gets fucking towed.

Another drunken shitbird dressed all in leather is standing at the bottom of the ramp to the law-enforcement building hollering at random cops as they go by... He opens up with "You fucking pussies! You're not so tough!"

One of the other cops says to me, "He must be talking about you."

I said, "No, I think he's talking about you, bro."

Not getting much of a response from the tired, trudging flatfoots, he ups the ante with the old standby: "You fucking pigs!"

One of the passing foot patrol officers says, "Man, that is so 1969. Can't you come up with something better?" The shitbird, speechless, staggers off to wherever he ends up spending the rest of his day; a bed, a gutter, maybe a vacant porta-potty.

Lights and siren across Sturgis once again for a stabbing at a Rally... but...Diverted to a medical call at a humongous saloon... other units were closer to the place, so they took it. Our call? Another drunk staggering around clutching his arm- broken for sure. What no one's sure about is how it happened. Fall off a bike? Trip and stumble? Shot off his mouth to the wrong people? He never tells us. Rally Rules: No ambulances go into a campground without cops to guard them. Two cars (four cops) respond to every medical call, for crowd control and to keep the milling mob from interfering with the medics.

Lights and siren back to Black Hawk- again. Three nights in a row the locals can't keep it in their pants... radio traffic of chokings and gun-waving were broadcast, resulting in four responding units and seven cops showing up. Once we took the whole thing apart and talked with everyone, it turned out to be all bullshit- just a garden variety neighborhood dispute between two drunk and probably mentally unbalanced people. Everyone involved was told to stop wasting our valuable time.

4. MONDAY

"*That disgusting bitch- I can't stand her.*" Can't we all just get along? Stay classy, Blackhawk. Four days, four neighborhood dispute/ assault calls.

***

A rider plowed his motorcycle into a tree, on the Tilford Service Road. One of his legs just "fell off" at the knee. The inmates of a nearby Rally campground came out to help, rigging an improvised pipe from a crushed beer can and gave him a big dose of weed …yes, marijuana…to ease his pain, so they said. Soon, two cops arrived. They were more practical, cinching a combat tourniquet on the poor bastard's leg-stump, so that he didn't bleed out before the Life Flight helicopter got there. This same bend in the service road has apparently claimed some unsuspecting gear-jammer every year. Can Rally campgrounds can get a "most likely to have an accident reconstruction done near you" award?

So the same local loser gets his name run on the radio and ticketed or arrested for something- three nights in a row. Maybe you should skip tonight and stay home, pal.

There is a back road into Sturgis from the Interstate that is a powerful draw to sneaky shitbirds. Unfortunately, for Rally week, it was guarded by something like six park rangers. Lots of Custer people seemed to like the shitbird shortcut. The rangers cited or arrested at least three people who were known Custer criminal celebrities.

Some crooks aren't very smart, but why would you go to a place where you know there are something like a hundred cops, and get drunk, stoned, and stupid? They all think they're the smart one, and they're slick enough to pull it off. Or, maybe they like the attention.

Your little novelty scooter might look like a Harley but... You probably don't get a lot of trim on Main Street by looking like a circus act. By the way, you probably shouldn't be riding it on a dark two-lane road with no tail or head light, at fifteen miles per hour, trying to hump your way up the canyon from Sturgis to Whitewood. One drunk in a pickup truck going your way? Blap! Nothing but a big grease spot, some teeth, and a mangled chain-wallet.

5. TUESDAY

A pickup truck caught on fire on the street in front of the Law Enforcement Building. The cops there used up every fire extinguisher on the first floor of the building, trying to put it out. "Goddamn", says somebody. "Isn't that what firefighters are for?" The hose-draggers showed up in time to save the axles, at least.

Seized from a lone vehicle driver during a traffic stop: Pills, hashish, pornography, and a large rubber ass... As in a set of replica buttocks, in their own carrying bag.

"Scattered thunderstorms" on the weather report during a summer in the Black Hills sometimes means brain-rattling rain for hours. It also meant a big hailstorm in the high country near Deadwood- state snow plows were called to plow the hail off the highway. Great motorcycle riding weather, eh?

Later, the rain slacked off, and the campground calls started. A lights-and-siren run to another mega-campground for a stroke victim. Crowd control while the ambulance crew does their business. Wandering drunks, screaming security people, revving bikes. Lights and siren back to town to clear the way through the head-light-to-tail-light traffic.

Much later, the sun sets and heavy fog settles. We watch "troopers in the mist"- the SD Highway Patrol is circling the highways east of Sturgis like sharks...so many cops in the area, we may have to start pulling each other over.

We try a few stops ourselves, but the radio pulls us back to the campgrounds. Mud, drunks, motorcycles, cars, a loud rock band, two beaten and bleeding people, no suspects, chaos and cop haters. Keep your backs to each other in this crowd. One "victim" was on federal probation, drunk and having neglected to let his parole officer know he'd left his home state. One bloody dude said he was jumped by three or four guys but could only describe one with white hair. So you probably mouthed off to a senior citizen and got tuned up for it huh? And we won't have to do a report, since your description sucks and there are no other witnesses? All right…everybody wins! Just another call at a *Legendary* campground.

We stayed up late into the morning hours, until four, covering the street. The two other patrol cars on duty roared off to the far north corner of the county for a fatal car wreck, leaving us to prowl the highways and campgrounds by ourselves.

It was worth staying late for the next call. We rolled to still another Rally campground for a woman with a broken leg. When we arrived we did some investigation and found that the injury was caused not by an assault but a drunken pole dancing accident. You can't make shit like that up.

We arrived back at the law enforcement center for some paperwork. I stood on the edge of the parking lot retaining wall and looked down at the street.

The arguing couple below the retaining wall at the law enforcement center didn't look up- they were working themselves into a domestic fight, or at least riding away drunk on their hog. Then the guy looked up, keys in hand, and decided to grab his old lady and walk down somewhere away from the area, at least until the cop up on the hill stopped watching him.

6. WEDNESDAY

"Earth is the insane asylum for the universe."
-A sign posted in the law enforcement dispatch center.

"Go Home Racist Pervert"
- Sign held by demonstrators at Ted Nugent concert.

"Hey, bro...how'd they know you were gonna be here?"
- One cop to another, after spotting the demonstrators' sign.

They started behind another quasi-outdoor tent-style mega-saloon ("*12,000 square feet of chaos and drama*" read the billboard). As they marched, they gathered speed and unfurled their banners. The ranks of watching cops tensed up...and smiled. Finally! They were supposed to start marching by six p.m., but they were running a bit late. Organizing a crowd of thirty (or maybe thirty-five) marchers takes time. There was some confusion as the mini-mob attempted to cross the busy four-lane highway, swelled with bike rally traffic, but no one got run over.

Across the street, their target: Another Bike Rally Mega-Saloon, and Uncle Ted Nugent, the Motor City Madman, the target of their wrath. His crime? Apparently, he said something bad about an ethnic group...or something. Diligent internet searching was unable to turn up any first-hand source of him daring to commit some kind of thought-crime...but somebody told somebody he did, and now they're on the march!

The crowd halted at the gates, having been briefed beforehand on the rules of the game: No blocking traffic, no trespassing on the saloon grounds. Twenty multi-agency cops and a milling crowd of orange-shirted security bozos kept things civil. The protestors unlimbered a bullhorn and a bunch of colorful signs. There was just one problem: the constant roar of Harleys all but drowned out the electronic lamenting.

Back on the road, more traffic stops. One, two… and our next contestant: We arrested him for DUI, Third Offense- a felony. Not a biker, but a local; a scummy old bum living out of his truck. His record showed *18 prior DUI convictions,* in his life. Maybe he has a small drinking problem.

In the booking room: A big, shirtless, barefoot guy with a ponytail: "Hey! I was in Sioux Falls, in the Pen, fuckers! You Indian haters are all the same. I'm from Pine Ridge and…"- looking at his arresting officer- "I'm going to kick the ass of *every* bald man in this room!"-and then looking at me- "Except for him. I *like* him!" Drunk, hamming it up for the female staff jail, playing the convict tough guy, not totally serious. He sat down and simmered down pretty fast.

Our sad drunk grew some balls and decided to pipe up about the unfairness of the situation. I looked him in the eye and politely suggested he mind his own business. He took the hint.

One sure way to keep your dispatchers happy: Go get pizza for them at Pizza Hut and bring it back. Mocha frappes from McDonalds do it, too. Rally is crunch time, and five dispatchers are crammed into a small radio room the size of a one-car garage, dealing with a constant stream of bewildering phone calls and garbled radio traffic. They need all the help they can get.

Backing up the Highway Patrol, in downtown Sturgis. Colorado dopers in trouble- boatload of cops for a little weed bust- one guy manned up and went to jail. Three adult brothers at the Rally with their 8-year old daughter…and weed. She was happy to talk to cops. She must be used to them by now. "It's like the fucking Old West here, this is bullshit!", said one of the clueless guys. "They make you pay cash for your tickets or they take you to jail! We're only one state away from Colorado, I can't believe it." Well, if you don't like it, Smiley, you can always go back to Colorado and stay there.

Overhead, the camera bird circles: A National Guard helicopter with an infrared camera, real-time-see-in-the-dark-video to the command post, and the computers and smartphones of all the cops. The Highway Patrol has extra cars, the SWAT team truck, and up-armored Humvees staged at the state highway shop. Overkill? The Big Brother Surveillance State? Well...this is a special event with four hundred thousand transients, and an unknown number of outlaw bikers and other escaped doorknobs in town for the next week, collectively packing enough booze, drugs, and firepower to overwhelm a small Central American country. Like they say, the rules are different for Rally Week.

The night: Campground fights, campground accidents, campground wrecks, drunken doofus mothers wandering around in confusion bellowing and staggering. Everyone playing biker dress-up, trying on their best "born to lose" act.

Hell's Half Hour: Bouncing from one campground to another, and to another and back again. Three crazy circuits on mud roads, county roads, on the highway. Noises: Traffic, revving cars, crazy bikes, radio calls about fights, drunks, dead bodies, and domestic disturbances, and more medical emergencies. About half of these calls are total bullshit or some strange misinterpretation of something someone half saw (a group of dipshits was strongly admonished for beating up a CPR dummy by the road, like it was a real person) but the other half ended up with lots of people going to jail and the hospital.

Case in point: An assault involving three or four people, one of one of whom panicked and drove away in his pickup truck, then rammed another car and attempted to flee the scene. He was apprehended by one of the other cops in the area...at first the call came in as three separate reports about three separate incidents but it turned out it was all done *by the same guy.* Aren't cell phones wonderful?

Friendly advice from Officer Friendly: If your parole officer tries to flag you down while you're driving, you probably shouldn't drive away from them and play stupid. Why? Well, when the *real police* show up and finally stop you with their big red and blue lights, your parole officer is likely to come up with someplace unpleasant for you to spend the rest of your weekend.

Woman scorned: Other deputies arrested a crazy screaming drunk chick at a campground. She was thrashing and kicking despite handcuffs and leg irons. One of the deputies sat in the backseat with her to keep her from kicking out the windows

(That's a good way to lose an ear and the tip of your nose when she bites it off in a frenzy.) It took a bunch of people to strap her into a rolling restraint chair at the jail and take her inside, banging her head on the headrest, screaming, out of her mind. Meth? PCP? Bath Salts or synthetics? Maybe, maybe not. It turned out her boyfriend of some years had revealed he was married with four kids and kicked her to the curb. The cops had to arrest her about the same time for a revoked driver's license and she went apeshit.

7. THURSDAY

"If I wake up in Detox, I'm going to kick somebody's ass!"
–A handcuffed drunk in the back seat of our patrol car.

I was on the Job today, before I even got in a patrol car. A one-vehicle rollover happened on the highway just up the road from my house, right in front of me. Two sobbing teenage boys clambered out, with cuts and bruises, but basically all right. Good on them for actually wearing their seatbelts. They were driving back home from the lake, got distracted and drove off a perfectly straight road…right in front of their mom, who was following them home in her car. Thankfully, she was much calmer than they were. I stayed there with them until the local cops showed up, then left. I was late for my "Real Job", but the boss understood.

First up: A Summerset property line dispute. The same old, *"the fence is three feet to the wrong side"* routine, topped with some intentional damage to said fence by the vehicle of one of the aggrieved parties, who then drove away. While we worked it out with the remaining complainant, the other half came rolling back home, with a 30-pack of Keystone Light in his back seat, and booze on his breath. After getting a handshake agreement on the fence matter, we adjourned to the second suspect's garage for some field sobriety tests- to the tune of *"Let the Good Times Roll"* by the Cars, on the guy's garage stereo. He wasn't there yet: a quick performance of the *"one drink away from disaster"* speech, while the guy sweated and trembled, and we cleared. Let the good times roll, indeed.

Back in Blackhawk: A trailer park meth guy freaking out at an ex-, ex-, ex-girlfriends' house. Hooked up to a SCRAM bracelet (tattles to his PO if he consumes alcohol, or is out after curfew, kind of like an invisible fence for scrotes) and shaking, nervous, jabbering, wandering around the trailer park in the dark. He took too many of someone else's prescription antidepressants by accident, thinking they were funny-shaped Advils. So he says, anyway. We talked him down, and convinced him to go in the ambulance to the nut ward. My partner had his Taser ready to give the guy some *Edison's Medicine*, if he got froggy, and I had my baton in hand, behind my back, ready to swing on him, *the old-fashioned way*. We might be nice guys, but we aren't stupid. He'll probably do a few days in jail after his PO finds out (of course, we called her) and gives him a piss test to see what he really ingested. The strapped-down meth head thanked me for being a *"cool cop"*. I pointed out that if he'd told me to go fuck myself or tried to fight us, his night would have ended much, much differently. This is called *education*.

Back in Sturgis, on random traffic stops. The odd couple: He's 4'10", she's 5'11"... On a bike together. They were coming from the one of the big Rally saloons. It was a good idea I didn't ask him if he was one of the midget wrestlers, because it turned out that he wasn't.

The drug bust: The city cops found weed, ice-clear, high-quality crystal meth, a High Point .380 pistol and a Mosin-Nagant rifle... it all started with a parking complaint in a downtown alley, and a couple of smarmy dopers who couldn't just move along when asked, but wanted to argue. There's a moral to this story, I'm sure.

A team of mega-campground "security" guards turned in a doper who had several glass Mason jars full of prime pot buds. He got dimed out because the campground people caught him drinking from a glass bottle of vodka. Glass bottles are verboten there. If he'd used plastic-bottle Vodka and plastic baggies for his dope he probably would have gotten away with it.

8. FRIDAY

When you make this many traffic stops in a week, and Rally Rules say pay cash tickets on the spot or go to jail, sometimes a little education and a written warning fits the situation better. The "no ticket" speech has been given about thirty times this week. "The three most important things at the Rally are: safety, safety, and safety. We want you to have an accident-free trip, so we can see you again next year..."

Another cop on the radio cleared his stop with *"Cited for littering and marijuana "* Aw, that could have been instant radio fame...insert the famous quote from the movie *Super Troopers*: *"Cited for littering and...littering and...smoking the reefer."* Other cops would have re-told that story at coffee breaks, for years. Totally worth an ass-chewing by the boss, if you ask me.

To another giant Rally campground we went, again with the ambulance, for a Roller Derby-related injury. It was no laughing matter. All right, maybe it was. One of the campground emergency medical techs gave us the patient update while waving a half-eaten piece of barbecue chicken around in one hand- it looked pretty good. It must be time for supper.

After our supper, we were back at the same mega-campground, again, this time in the dark. Picture the same chaos as previous medical calls there- but wait! Could somebody please tell me why those doorknobs in the golf cart speeding up to the first-aid station are wearing superhero costumes? And how did one of them fall off a retaining wall and get a compound fracture of their forearm? Alcohol may have been involved. We helped load the patient and I helped the ambulance back out. Totally routine, for Rally. Then, I shooed a golf cart full of midget wrestlers away from being crushed by the backing ambulance. Luckily, we left the area without crushing the little grapplers any shorter.

Blackhawk again? Why, *yes*. Four cars running hot to deal with a knife-waving thirteen-year-old. Strangely, the locals here don't take Rally Week off...they just keep on doing what they *always* do. Luckily, no one got cut, or shot when it was all over.

In downtown Sturgis at bar closing time. Crowds in the street, people milling around, blocking traffic, yelling. Is it a fight? We stop to investigate and find nothing but a big mass of confused drunken morons ejected from the bars at closing time with no plan. On a second pass, I use the loudspeaker to politely tell more wandering drunks to stay out of traffic. Two black dudes on the sidewalk yelling: "Fuck the police!" Really? No doubt they believe us cops are racist because we're always harassing them for no reason...except for attracting attention to themselves by hollering the F-bomb. I gave them a jaunty wave and a cheesy smile...and we drove away from their dumb asses, leaving them looking confused. We called for help, the city cops appeared, did nothing and disappeared- the crowd stayed in the street. We looked at each other and motored away. Fuck it. It's a "city problem".

9. SATURDAY

The cops here call it "Sucker Punch Saturday", due to the tendency of the locals and the bikers to whip on each other for no reason on the last "official" day of Rally Week. It's surmised everyone suddenly realizes the fun is almost over and decides to make up for lost time by drinking, whoring, and fighting just a bit more.

We stopped two French nationals, speeding down a lonely two-lane road on their rented bikes, in the middle of nowhere. Our "parlez-vous" was poor but French Dude #2 spoke German...my high-school Deutsch was a little rusty, but we were making some progress. My partner was more direct. French Dude#1's "*No speaka de English*" act evaporated at my partner's use of the magic word "*Jail*." Suddenly, we were very easy to understand. Once we got that settled, they were sent packing with a just a written warning.

A radio call of two silver Chevy Silverado pickups speeding down I-90: Both apparently contained passengers drinking road beers. What are the odds? Apparently, pretty good, since we saw one pass us going the other way, with no safe way to turn around on him.

Bad weather started rolling in. The sunset sky darkened dramatically, and lightning flashed from the higher Hills. Before the rain started there was another traffic stop at a convenience store parking lot with a slightly impaired guy and his girlfriend. Once again, *one drink away from disaster*. A cash speeding ticket, a quick trip to a nearby ATM, and we sent them across the parking lot to a nearby steakhouse to have supper and sober up.

The big storm cut loose with tons and tons of rain and wind. A lull on the radio for a few hours, and then the mean drunks came out swinging.

We bounced up to Sturgis, just in time to turn around and roar back down the valley, to Blackhawk for a reported fight and a DUI motorist in a parking lot. We ended up right in front of the fire station (And Sheriff's substation, very convenient). It was a complicated drama where we finally ended up arresting a 20-year-old crying female drunk.

While we did our field sobriety tests, and arranged for her car to be taken away, two other units and four other cops ran hot to a call of a suicidal man with a shotgun, holed up in his house, right in scenic Blackhawk. The address sounded close, but I wasn't familiar with the area. I heard sirens approaching us. Louder, louder, louder.

THUMP!

Shit, was that a gunshot? Turns out it was, and close, too. The suicidal guy in question learned the cops were coming to get him, decided *tonight* wasn't the night, and walked outside to give up. He couldn't figure out how to unload his shotgun in the dark, so he fired the chambered shell into the ground by his porch. There are *so* many ways that could have gone badly for him, but it didn't. Good thing for him he didn't see our lights and decide to saunter over to us, just so he could give himself up, cradling a loaded shotgun in one arm.

Jail: Bright lights, radio chatter, bleach smell. A potluck with sloppy joes was going on in the jail control room for a retiring jailer hanging it up after her twentieth Rally. There were desserts, too.

"This is a good cookie", said one of the cops, while he munched on a treat and watched a TV monitor picture of a thrashing, moaning drunk strapped into the "angry chair" in an isolation cell. The moaning drunk turned into a yelling drunk, got louder, thrashed around more and more...and then passed out. Another Rally rock concert casualty, brought in for drinking and fighting.

Two plainclothes drug cops came in dragging a tall drunk woman. She was a looker, but had a big mouth. After a lot of bad noise, she squared off with a female jailer, began crying, and fed her a sad (and likely coached) tale of woe about her medical infirmities, including a plate in her head, and concluded by saying she couldn't be admitted to jail without going to the hospital first to be medically cleared. The jailer sent them all away. The narcs dragged her off, disgusted, for an emergency room checkup, and then maybe a readmission to the jail. Which brings up an interesting question: If you are too fragile to sit in jail, aren't you too fragile to be drinking and abusing drugs in public on a Saturday night?

Full moon Saturday night: The last night of the Rally. Tomorrow will surely be the death of fun. *Get it on while you still can.* Mean drunks emptied liquor bottles, downed fistfulls of pills and whipped on each other in the muddy shambles of their campgrounds, surrounded by passed-out casualties, uprooted tents, and wrecked bikes. Soon, though, the gaps between outbursts got longer. The night's constant stream of chatter on the police radio slowed, and then paused.

I fire up a Cohiba cigar and sit down on the top of the retaining wall at the Law Enforcement Center. It's 2 a.m., again. Through billowing blue clouds of aromatic smoke, I scope out the Sturgis street scene down below and hum *The Wind Cries Mary,* by Jimi Hendrix, under my breath. It seems to fit the mood.

It's like watching the fairgrounds as the carnival packs up-a little lonely, a little sad. The tow trucks and the city police foot patrol teams prowl Main Street Sturgis one last time, and dragoon a few more unsuspecting overnight parkers. The garbage trucks rev up their engines, the seedy local taxis make their ceaseless circles looking for the last late drunks.

The lady bartenders straggle down the street in their tawdry little outfits while the big inflatable Jack Daniels bottle on the roof of one of the bars begins to deflate and sag. The city crews are folding up the photo towers and traffic barricades... The last few wandering drunks stagger around aimlessly in circles, staring, mumbling, and clutching at themselves.

The city cops' temporary Rally foot teams de-mobilize... they jump into their personal cars, disbanding and dissipating like an organism dissolving in acid. Our patrol car crews shove things into kit-bags and turn in our borrowed radios and uniform shirts. What were tight cohesive units, are now scattered to the four winds after nine days of artificial life.

Back inside, a round of handshakes between all the cops in the squad room, with lots of backslapping, teasing and ball-busting. We scarf down some last cold cut sandwiches, grab our commemorative Jack Daniels bottles and Sturgis Rally Police pins-to show the rest of the cop-world we'd "been there, done that"-and then everyone scatters for another year.

The Rally of the Damned is over.

STREET LIFE

DEATH IN A COW PASTURE

I got called out to work twenty minutes early and raced away from my house with lights and siren clearing my way through the early spring afternoon. I pushed my black Dodge Durango Pursuit to one hundred and kept it there.

The accident scene was about thirty miles away and when I arrived, two state troopers and two fire trucks were there already. The LifeFlight helicopter had landed in the cow pasture a short distance away from the blacktopped two-lane highway to the reservation, its rotors stopped and the crew milling around. They weren't in a hurry to take off again. Red, blue and amber lights sparkled and flashed. Radios crackled with terse, laconic messages.

A cheap, white, ten-year-old Chevrolet sedan lay on its side in the pasture, the roof bent into a funny shape from numerous impacts with the dirt. It had no license plates and a temporary registration, as it had just been purchased, probably with a tax refund or monthly check. A heap of blankets lay by the side of the Chevy, covering the guest of honor: a thirty-year-old prison parolee with a no-bond warrant for his arrest. That was the least of his problems, now.

The troopers investigated the crash, one of our sergeants and I investigated the man's death. Weird, how we have these little rules of ours that try to segregate chaos into neat categories. The county coroner showed up in his Dodge Power Wagon and his cowboy boots. The coroner gig was only part-time, as he was a rancher by trade. He always had a calm, friendly manner in the middle of disasters and I liked working death scenes with him. I took notes and pictures as he pulled the blankets aside to examine the dead man.

The dead man was still staring. He had various emergency

medical devices, tubes and other things still stuck in him, evidence of the fire fighters' short but intense battle to keep him alive. It hadn't been enough. The dead man's car had left the road at a very high speed, turned sideways, dug its wheels into the dirt and began rolling. And rolling. And rolling. Somewhere in the spin cycle, the dead man parted ways with the car through a window. The car didn't care and kept going without him, striking him with its tires in passing and injuring him more as both continued their trajectory into the cow pasture. Objects in motion tend to remain in motion: Physics. Simple, cruel physics.

Artifacts of the car's ballistic trip into the pasture included broken glass, pieces of trim, loose papers, an empty traveler of Captain Morgan, and the remains of a Hardee's fish sandwich. It was the Friday a week before Easter- maybe the dead man was Catholic. Maybe he just liked fish sandwiches. A search of the car later found that he definitely liked liquor, cocaine, weed and rap CD's. Bone Thugs and Tupac, to be exact. Live like a thug, die like a thug, as they say.

The dead man looked much older than his driver's license photo. Some cop consternation ensued for a while as we tried to match tattoos with criminal histories, tried to contact someone at the state pen to verify a picture. Later in the day, we decided it was the right guy. I guess sudden, violent death can age you a bunch. Maybe doing a couple two-three years in the pen and absconding from parole can age you, too.

Eventually, the coroner gave his verdict: death by blunt-force trauma from a motor vehicle accident. No surprise there. Despite all his other mistakes, the dead guy might have lived if he'd just snapped on his seat belt. Car crashes are a lot more survivable if you don't leave the car partway through.

The fire guys eventually all begged off, picked up their gear and left the scene. The helicopter spooled up its engines and fled in a cloud of rotor noise and burned jet-fuel smell. A local rancher showed up to help fix the fence the Chevy had plowed through on its short trip to oblivion. A local TV news crew showed up but kept their distance from the scene. One of the troopers' bosses went to give them a stand-up interview.

We sacked the dead man up in a body bag. Our usual tough-guy banter and cop-to-cop ball-busting stilled. Fuckup or not, this guy was something to somebody, somewhere. We lifted him into the back of the coroner's Power Wagon for the trip to the morgue in the big city. We all stood there quiet for a moment: a rancher with a cowboy hat, a coroner with his cowboy boots, the state troopers in their spiffy uniforms and Smokey Bear hats, us deputies in our black-and-tan outfits with body armor over the top. Someone gave the sign of the cross, quickly, furtively, like a kid whistling past the graveyard.

The mood broke. One cop started giving another one shit about something and we shifted into the next step of the process- sifting through the ruined Chevy and waiting for the tow truck to cart it away. The coroner left in his Power Wagon with the dead man in the back. A trooper followed in his car, to maintain the chain of custody, for legal reasons. Order out of chaos. Hopefully, in time for lunch.

Watching the little funeral procession leave, it occurred to me that, sometimes, people blithely talk about Western South Dakota as "part of the Midwest" and refer to various towns here as "Midwestern towns", and talk about "Midwestern values". That makes us sound like we grow corn and walk around saying, "Oh, yah", and "You betcha".

Bullshit.

The Black Hills and the Badlands are most definitely The West. Sometimes they are still the Old West. Cowboys and Indians still roam the highways, not on horses, but in pickup trucks and cheap white Chevy's they just bought with their tax refund. And if they die in a cow pasture by the side of the highway after they get bucked off their horse or ejected from their white Chevy, their mortal remains could take that last trip to town in the back of a pickup truck driven by a man wearing cowboy boots.

If that's not Western, what is?

TWO WORLDS

My family and I wandered into our favorite pizza place, one summer afternoon only to find...the Governor.

He was eating his pizza with a fork...and a knife. His skinny, bird-like, white legs were crossed like a woman's, with his flip-flops dangling from their straps. His plain white t-shirt read "LIVE UNITED". Drinking a horse-piss-tasting Corona, he was in Norwegian nirvana, while he chatted with his wife and a couple of cronies. Probably a nice guy, but kind of fruity, by the standards of the western part of our state.

I thought about the Governor a couple of days later, when a cop friend of mine called to tell me Buffalo Puncher had been arrested again. Puncher had been a fixture of my night-shift police world in the old days. A strapping six-foot-three lad, built like the sometime logger and mostly convict that he was, he had a prodigious appetite for drink, drugs, and disorderly conduct. I dubbed him "Buffalo Puncher", the very night I first met him-he was dead drunk in the downtown area, at 3 A.M., punching a decorative plastic buffalo in the snout. A real classy guy.

I once arrested him for driving drunk in a dark alley, after catching him speeding on an ancient three-wheeled all-terrain-vehicle, with no lights, no license, and a bag of marijuana in his pocket. He was very casual about the arrest and the trip to jail. It was business as usual, for him, and for me, too.

This time, though, my cop friend told me Puncher had gotten strung out on "spice", a synthetic PCP-like stimulant, went off his nut and got pig-piled by four cops, hog-tied, and taken to jail. He was already on parole from his latest bounce to the state pen, for distribution of a controlled substance-and for violating his parole by bringing methamphetamine into the minimum-security unit he'd finally conned his way into. His new charges of ingestion of a controlled substance, and four counts of assault on police officers probably wasn't going to look good at his parole revocation hearing. Another parole revocation hearing, just like the others before.

Buffalo Puncher and the Governor didn't have a lot in common. I don't know if Puncher ate his pizza with his hands, but I was there the night he almost lost one of them after punching a glass-fronted cabinet in a drunken frenzy, during a vicious fight with some of his "friends". The emergency room docs sewed him up, but he almost died anyway, from blood loss.

The Governor had decided that he needed to do something about people like Buffalo Puncher, though. He and his cronies were apparently distressed that too many "drug offenders" like Puncher were needlessly spending their time in prison, rather than being productive members of society. A couple of years prior, they had pushed through sweeping reforms to do more "community-based corrections", and more "treatment" of drug offenders. What it mostly translated into was more chances to attend parole hearings…more chances for guys like Puncher to fuck up without really getting locked up. Critics suggested the Governor and his buddies were just trying to get free federal money and put off building or expanding the state's prison system. The critics were probably right.

Regardless of the reasons, the reforms were done with good will and the best of intentions. Lots of sensitive people cooed and made concerned faces through their sensitive squeezy-glasses while they bloviated about poor people like Puncher, who didn't need to be in prison…and we would be more progressive and stuff by keeping them in the "community" (whatever that meant), with their families. Puncher probably liked that part. He could stay out on the street with his ex-con, druggie brother, his illegitimate kid (who he paid no child support to), and his doting, addled mother (who blamed the police and a lack of drug-treatment money, rather than her own drug use and shitty parenting skills).

So, a convicted felon, who'd been given a lot of chances to fuck up, (reduced and dropped charges, suspended imposition of sentences, informal diversion, probation, parole, drug treatment, minimum security work-release) took them all…and continued to fuck up. And here he was again, fighting with the cops, while the sensitive people like the Governor sipped their Coronas and crossed their legs, and ate pizza with a fork and knife, and talked about the community, and felt real good about "living united".

The Governor and Buffalo Puncher live in two different worlds. It's a mistake to believe that these two worlds share any of the same values or morals. It's a mistake to apply the values and morals of the Governor's world to Buffalo Puncher's world.

His world doesn't care.

FREE ADVICE

Here's a few tips for you prospective young criminals, in a sort of free-form verse:

If you are out driving around bored at night, don't bring a cooler of beer with you

If you bring a cooler of beer, don't bring your grand paw's guns

If you bring grand paw's guns, don't shoot them randomly in the dark

If you shoot randomly in the dark, don't kill someone's cow

If you kill someone's cow, don't get your car stuck trying to leave

If you get your car stuck, don't try to summon help by knocking on the door of a

Suspicious little old lady

BUT… If you knock on the door of a suspicious old lady, don't call your drunk friend to

Come pick you up

If you call your drunk friend to pick you up, tell your drunk friend not to try out-running

The cops by driving into a field and turning off his lights

Homeland security grants mean even podunk cops have night vision goggles to see you

If all of the above fails and you are caught by the cops

Try not to bounce your bag of weed off your foot as you try to ditch it

And don't do it in front of a running car video camera

Everyone will call you a dumbass

And they'll be right.

ABOUT THE AUTHOR

Seth Thompson

Seth Thompson spent nearly three decades at numerous adult baby-sitting jobs: city cop, correctional officer, park ranger, deputy sheriff and a bunch of private security jobs that sounded way more thrilling than they really were. He is now retired from patrol work and is spending his time teaching good people how to shoot, writing, and discovering there really is life after being a cop.

Thompson lives with his family in rural Custer County, South Dakota, where bison and cattle still out-number people.

All entries from the Custer County Sheriff's Log were previously published in the *Custer County Chronicle*, from 2005-2014 and appear with permission, as well as *Welcome To The Night Shift, Dealing With A Flashlight Problem, Warning: Reading This Column May Cause Drowsiness, The Street Cop's Superstition Sweepstakes, A Preemptive Apology for 2010, You Say You Want A Revolution?, Lumpy Gives Fire Directions, Lumpy Says Goodbye To The Crown Vic,* and *One In Five.*

Rally Of The Damned, Death In A Cow Pasture, Two Worlds, and *Free Advice* are previously unpublished.

Get in touch with the author: seth@sheriffslog.com

Check out the website and get Seth's weekly newsletter: sheriffslog.com

Find the author on FaceBook:
https://www.facebook.com/profile.php?id=61560987152314

Get the current Sheriff's Log and other news and views at the *Custer County Chronicle:* https://www.custercountychronicle.com/

Made in the USA
Middletown, DE
12 January 2025